Pathfinder®Guides

North Wales and Snowdonia

Walks

Compiled by
Terry Marsh

Contents

At-a-glance

Comments

There are impressive views of Llandudno, along the coast and across the Conwy Estuary to the mountains of Snowdonia on this short circuit of the Great Orme.

As well as Hope Mountain, there are distant views of the Dee estuary on this undemanding walk in the valley of the River Alyn.

The life of Lloyd George, a ruined medieval castle and grand coastal views are the chief ingredients of this easy walk in the Lleyn Peninsula.

A simple and straightforward amble along both sides of the Afon Clwyd, linking the coastal resort of Rhyl with inland Rhuddlan; plenty of scope for observing birdlife along the way.

Pleasant walking in the valley of the Afon Ystrad is followed by great views of Denbigh Castle across the Vale of Clwyd.

A straightforward stroll along the Llangollen Canal to reach the magnificent Pontcysyllte Aqueduct.

Extending the traditional walk to view the Aber Falls, this route makes use of the North Wales Path to visit Aber's lesser-known falls.

A stiff climb out of Penmaenmawr to the prehistoric Druid's Circle is rewarded by superb views, both along the coast, and inland to the Carneddau.

The dominating feature of this walk is Telford's majestic Pontcysyllte Aqueduct, which carries the Shropshire Union Canal over the Dee valley.

A walk through the parkland of Chirk Castle is followed by a dramatic descent into the lovely Ceiriog valley. Near the end you pass beneath an adjacent viaduct and aqueduct.

From this most northerly section of the Clwydian mountain range, the views extend over Prestatyn and Rhyl, and along the coast to Llandudno and Great Orme.

On this circuit of Llyn Padarn there are fine views of Snowdon, attractive woodland sections, relics of the Llanberis slate quarry industry, a medieval castle and pleasant walking beside a lake.

You can expect steep climbs and rough going in places on this itinerary across Yr Eifl and its neighbouring peaks. But the isolation of the peninsula brings with it a keen sense of openness.

From the encircling walls of a fine medieval town, the walk progresses onto the panoramic heights of Conwy Mountain, before seeking a way back to Conway through farmland pastures.

An easy but rambling circular walk starting from the popular Loggerheads Country Park, and following in the footsteps of Felix Mendelssohn, the German composer.

This approach to Moel Famau is circuitous, starting to the south and following 'The Mushroom Path'. Eventually, the route joins Offa's Dyke Path, to the summit of the hill, before a descent through woodland.

After a gentle walk from Beddgelert, the walk climbs through heathered slopes into the hidden glen Cwm Bychan, film setting for *The Inn of the Sixth Happiness*, followed by a finish through the Aberglaslyn Pass.

With such far-reaching views, it's easy to see why the Clwydian Hills were favoured for the route of Offa's Dyke; this walk follows well-defined tracks, and visits two Iron Age hill forts.

A steep but immensely pleasurable linear ascent to a seldom-visited and stunning viewpoint overlooking Anglesey and the North-West Wales coast.

This relatively easy ascent of Tal y Fan rewards you with magnificent views of the Eastern Carneddau and the distant southern summits of Snowdonia. Expect boggy and indistinct paths once you leave the summit.

This splendid coastal walk takes you around the tip of the Lleyn Peninsula, following in the footsteps of medieval pilgrims on their way to Bardsey Island.

A superb ramble into a rarely visited nook of the Eastern Carneddau, far from the outside world, and into a realm of former industry.

The lakes are popular all year round, but few visitors venture far from the shorelines; make the most of the stunning landscapes on this circular walk.

This lengthy but easy circuit of Llyn Brenig romps across heathland and through part of the Clocaenog Forest, with extensive views of the heather moorlands of Mynydd Hiraethog.

A splendid up and down route, often steep, across heather uplands leads to a more relaxed return above the valley of the Afon Morwynion.

A walk that really does have everything: a climb that comes right at the beginning, spectacular scenery, historic attractions and a relaxing finale along a canal towpath.

Putting you within striking distance of two of the Berwyns highest summits, the half way point of this walk is a distinct pass that penetrates the wide ridge.

Easy, but not easy; this ascent of Snowdon is a route less travelled than others, but has a magical appeal about it, and a fine finish that treks a rarely visited ridge and crosses the scene of Man's industrial past.

The sands of Newborough, Anglesey, from the summit of Mynydd Mawr

Introduction to North Wales and Snowdonia

The companion volume in the *Pathfinder®* series – Snowdonia – focuses exclusively on the National Park. This North Wales and Snowdonia title still retains walks in the National Park, including another ascent of Snowdon itself, and extends eastwards to embrace the less well-known, but highly attractive countryside of north-east Wales that lies between Snowdonia and the English border: the Berwyn mountains, the Clwydian Hills and the Vale of Clwyd. It also includes walks on the Lleyn Peninsula.

North-East Wales

This is a region of hills and vales, moorlands and forests, rather than mountains, although the smooth, grassy slopes of the Berwyns rise to over 2,700ft (822m) as they sweep across the area to the east of Bala Lake to descend into the Vale of Llangollen. To the north of Llangollen, beyond the Horseshoe Pass, the broad and fertile Vale of Clwyd stretches to the North Wales holiday coast and the reclaimed marshlands of the Morfa Rhuddlan. To the west the Vale is bordered by the moorlands of Mynydd Hiraethog, partially covered by the conifers of Clocaenog Forest. To the east is the switchback range of the Clwydian Hills, rising to 1,818ft (554m) at Moel Famau and providing a succession of magnificent viewpoints over the Vale. Threading its way across the ridge of the Clwydians is one of the most spectacular sections of Offa's Dyke Path National Trail, which provides opportunities for energetic but highly scenic and enjoyable walking before it descends to the coast

The spectacular Aber Falls

at Prestatyn.

To the east of the Clwydians, rolling country leads to the Dee and the English border. In the Middle Ages, Chester, the major town on the River Dee, was the launching pad for successive English invasions of North Wales and the narrow coastal strip was the easiest way in. A whole series of castles line this route, including the first two built by Edward I at Flint and Rhuddlan – during the course of his successful conquest of Wales in the late 13th century, forerunners of the great castles that surround Snowdonia. Another outstanding castle is the border fortress at Chirk, continually modernised and occupied since it was built.

Apart from the medieval castles, other historic monuments range from prehistoric hill forts to the beautifully situated ruins of Valle Crucis Abbey, and from the cathedral at St Asaph to various industrial remains. The Industrial Revolution has left its mark on parts of north-east Wales, and no visitor can fail to be impressed by Thomas Telford's soaring aqueducts at Pontcysyllte and Chirk.

Snowdonia

Here can be found some of the most spectacular scenery in Britain and presiding imperially over this array of jagged ridges and formidable-looking peaks is Yr Wyddfa, the highest mountain in Britain south of the Scottish Highlands. It is known by its more familiar name, allegedly bestowed upon it by Dark Age sailors, who when voyaging from Ireland to Wales saw snow-covered hills on the skyline and christened them the Snowy Hills or 'Snaudune', initially a collective name that later became restricted to the highest peak only.

Snowdonia can be divided into a number of clearly defined ranges, each with their own characteristics. By far the most popular and most frequently climbed are the Carneddau, the Glyders and Snowdon itself in the north of the region. The great ridges and sweeping grassy slopes of the Carneddau cover an extensive area between the Conwy valley and Nant Ffrancon, and in the north descend abruptly to the coast. Between the Nant Ffrancon and Llanberis passes rise the majestic Glyders, their shattered volcanic rocks providing the spectacular pinnacles and formations that litter the summits of Glyder Fawr and Glyder Fach.

Beyond Llanberis Pass is Snowdon itself, accessible from a number of routes, and to the west of Snowdon lies the Hebog range. The central zone of Snowdonia comprises the shapely mass of Moel Siabod between the Llugwy and Lledr valleys, the Moelwyns and Cnicht, the latter sometimes known as the 'Welsh Matterhorn'.

As well as mountain climbs the region has plenty of easy low-level walks. Separating the ranges are delightful valleys, like the steep-sided gorges of the Llugwy and Lledr near Betws-y-Coed and the wider Vale of Ffestiniog. Scattered throughout the area are lakes of varying size. Among the most beautiful of these are Tal-y-llyn and the Cregennen lakes overlooked by Cadair Idris, Llyn y Gader below the western flanks of Snowdon, Llyn Ogwen dramatically situated between the Glyders and the Carneddau, and Llynnau Mymbyr near Capel Curig, from whose shores there is possibly the finest view of all of Snowdon.

When travelling through Snowdonia the foremost historic remains that catch the eye are the great medieval castles, among the finest in Europe. Some of these were built by the native Welsh princes, as at Dolwyddelan, reputed birthplace of Llewellyn the Great, and Dolbadarn, but most were built by Edward I.

In order to consolidate his conquest of Wales, Edward encircled Snowdonia with the formidable and highly expensive castles of Conwy, Beaumaris, Caernarfon and Harlech, all embodying the latest sophistications of castle construction. These castles remain as examples of medieval military architecture at its most advanced and refined. By far the most striking and large-scale man-made intrusions on the landscape of Snowdonia have come from 19th- and 20th-century industrial and commercial developments. Foremost among these was the slate quarrying industry which reached its peak at the end of the 19th century. It has now largely disappeared but around Llanberis and Blaenau Ffestiniog the remains of that industry have been turned into fascinating tourist attractions.

In 1951, as a recognition of its unique landscape value, Snowdonia became one of Britain's first national parks.

Walking in the area

With its magnificent and varied scenery and wealth of historic attractions, it is not surprising that North Wales is one of the most popular walking destinations in Britain. In the following selection of routes, the aim has been to include all aspects of the landscape of the region and to provide a balance of easy, moderate and more challenging walks. So take your pick. At one end of the spectrum is an entirely flat walk beside the Afon Clwyd from Rhyl to Rhuddlan; at the other is a lengthy and demanding ascent of Snowdon itself, from Rhyd Ddu, a route less well-used.

Read carefully the general descriptions of each of the walks, and the distances and approximate times, and choose those which best suit your interests, level of ability and fitness, the amount of time available, and – above all – the state of the weather, and enjoy exploring this wonderful area in the best possible way, on foot.

This book includes a list of waypoints alongside the description of the walk, so that you can enjoy the full benefits of gps should you wish to. For more information on using your gps, read the Pathfinder® Guide *GPS for Walkers*, by gps teacher and navigation trainer, Clive Thomas (ISBN 978-0-7117-4445-5). For essential information on map reading and basic navigation, read the Pathfinder® Guide *Map Reading Skills* by author of this guide, Terry Marsh (ISBN 978-0-7117-4978-8). Both titles are available in bookshops or can be ordered online at www.pathfinderwalks.co.uk

Short walks up to 2½ hours

Looking across to the Clwydian Hills from near Rhuddlan

Great Orme

		GPS waypoints	
Start	Great Orme Country Park, signposted from centre of Llandudno. Alternatively come on either the Cabin Lift or Tramway from Llandudno	☑ SH 765 833 Ⓐ SH 774 829 Ⓑ SH 770 838 Ⓒ SH 757 840	
Distance	3¼ miles (5.25km)		
Height gain	625 feet (190m)		
Approximate time	2 hours		
Parking	Car park at start		
Route terrain	Undulating rocky and grassy landscapes; some road walking		
Ordnance Survey maps	Landranger 115 (Snowdon/Yr Wyddfa), Explorer OL17 (Snowdon/Yr Wyddfa)		

The familiar and distinctive headland of the Great Orme rises to 679ft (207m) above the elegant resort of Llandudno and its summit, from where the walk starts, can be reached by chairlift and tramway from the town centre as well as by car. Most of it is now a country park and on this short circuit there is a succession of outstanding views that take in Llandudno and its curving bay, the Conwy Estuary, mountains of Snowdonia, the Menai Strait and the island of Anglesey. Historic interest is provided by the Great Orme Mines and St Tudno's Church.

As well as the superb views, attractions on the Great Orme range from Bronze Age copper mines and a Dark Age Christian site to the Edwardian tramway, first opened in 1902, and modern chairlift and dry ski-slope.

☑ Head for the Visitor Centre and turn down the road, tramway on your left. Join the grassy path to the right of the road; as the road bends left this path continues down alongside a wall (marked by low marker posts with a white 'walker' on), shortly passing a Great Orme Historical Trail Information Board. At a fingerpost in bracken, keep right to drop to a tarred lane just above the Great Orme Mines. These are old copper mines, first worked in at least 1580BCE and as such the oldest known metal-working site in Britain. Turn right, ignore the left fork to the mine and shortly bend left along the roughening track that passes above the Visitor Centre. Remain on this track through a metal gate and past houses. Go ahead on the tarred lane and bear left to reach a junction Ⓐ at St Beunos Road and the main road carrying the steep tram tracks.

Turn left uphill, go through the gate beside a cattle-grid and then turn right, cross the tramway and walk along the rough lane signed as a footpath for St Tudno's Church. At the fork in 50 paces,

St Tudno's Church

through bracken. This cuts through to a sheep-cropped grass common; bear right up across this to find a gravel lane and turn right, shortly picking up a stone estate wall on your left. This is your constant companion for the remainder of the walk. There are excellent views across the Irish Sea; on very clear days the Isle of Man and the Lake District's mountains can be seen.

At a wall corner **C** turn left, continue beside it and follow it as it curves left again. Now come possibly the finest views of the walk, looking across the Conwy Estuary to Conwy town and castle, with the panorama of the Snowdonia mountains visible on the horizon to the south.

keep right on the gravel lane, walking through to a turning area at Pink Farm. Look right here for a kissing-gate and multiple fingerposts, go through this and turn left. Pass through a metal gate behind the farm and cottage and go ahead along a fenced track. Passing a field gate, this narrows to a path; go through two kissing-gates and keep ahead to reach a lane and St Tudno's Church **B**.

Turn uphill and wind with the road above the sloping graveyards. About 50yds beyond the upper boundary wall, fork right through some roadside boulders onto a wide grassy path

Keep beside the wall where it turns left again and head uphill to return to the start.

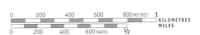

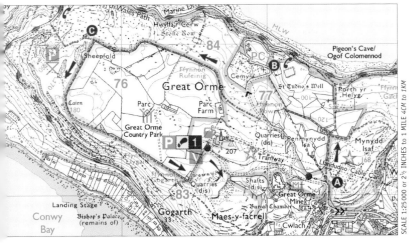

Caergwrle and Hope

		GPS waypoints
Start	Caergwrle	
Distance	3¾ miles (6km)	☑ SJ 305 574
Height gain	375 feet (115m)	Ⓐ SJ 311 576
		Ⓑ SJ 310 583
Approximate time	2 hours	Ⓒ SJ 321 587
Parking	Car park at start	Ⓓ SJ 324 585
Route terrain	Woodland; some road walking	Ⓔ SJ 318 576
Ordnance Survey maps	Landranger 117 (Chester and Wrexham), Explorer 256 (Wrexham & Llangollen)	

Towards the end of this pleasant and easy walk in the Alyn valley, there are fine views of the wooded slopes of Hope Mountain. On such a modest walk there should be enough energy at the end to take you up to the ruins of Caergwle castle; it's a grand viewpoint.

☑ Begin by turning left out of the car park along High Street and take the first turning on the right, passing to the right of a church. Follow a narrow lane to a road, cross over and continue along a tarmac track which descends to cross a 17th-century packhorse bridge over the River Alyn. Head uphill between houses and cottages, cross a railway line and descend to a road.

Walk ahead up the concrete drive opposite. Near the top, look on your right for steps up to a kissing-gate, go through this and turn left. Walk outside the property boundary to another kissing-gate ahead. Go through this and turn left along a fenced path Ⓐ. Remain on this path which shortly skirts a line of trees. This is the line of Wat's Dyke. Like the better-known and more extensive Offa's Dyke, this was constructed in the 8th or 9th century as a boundary between the Kingdom of Mercia and the Welsh.

Through a kissing-gate and remain with the fenced path, rising beside a driveway to a road. Turn left, take the first turning on the left and follow a lane up to Hope church. In front of the medieval church turn right along a track Ⓑ to the road, cross over and take the tarmac track opposite. Just after passing a farm, turn left, at a public footpath sign, descend to a stile, climb it and bear right to head diagonally uphill across a field. Descend to climb another stile, and turn right along the right-hand edge of two fields, to another stile. After the next stile, keep along the left edge of the field, turn right in the corner and look for another stile on your left. Cross this and go ahead to a further stile giving onto a grassy track. Keep ahead through a gate, past a cottage to a lane Ⓒ.

Turn right along this and after 400yds – just after passing a large brick house (Shordley Hall) on the left – turn right over a stile Ⓓ and walk across a field to a metal gate. Go through, continue across the next field, climb a stile and keep ahead to join and keep

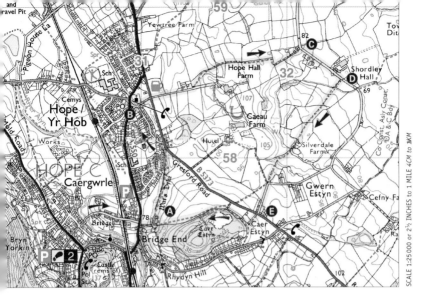

| 0 | 200 | 400 | 600 | 800 METRES | 1 | KILOMETRES |
| 0 | 200 | 400 | 600 YARDS | ½ | | MILES |

alongside the left field edge. Go through a gate near the field corner, head diagonally across the next field and descend to go through a gate. Walk the track past ruins and through another gate. As the track turns left, look carefully on your right for a curious stile across sheathed barbed wire hidden in overgrown bushes. Walk along the right edge of the pasture to a point 30 paces beyond the second pylon; here fork half-left up the bank, pass through the line of old hedge and continue half-right to an unusual three-way stile in the field corner. Bear right along the lane to reach a T-junction **E**. Cross the main road and climb the stile opposite. Walk along the right-hand edge of a field, pass through a hedge gap and keep ahead to the edge of the wooded hill of Caer Estyn, the site of an Iron Age hill fort.

Turn right through two kissing-gates in quick succession and keep along the left edge of a field below the wooded hill. Through another kissing-gate, cross the quarry road and take a kissing-gate into a fenced path that continues to skirt the foot of Caer Estyn.

This gradually descends the field edge, with good views ahead across Caergwrle and the Alyn valley to Hope Mountain, right to Hope church and the distant industrial complexes of Deeside.

The path drops to reach the stile near to the point **A** used earlier in the walk. Through the kissing-gate and descend alongside the boundary fence ahead to find the steps down to a concrete drive. Walk down to the road and turn left. Go across the river bridge beside **The Bridge** pub and cross carefully to the right. Pass beneath the railway bridge and turn right along Castle Street. Stay on this to the T-junction with High Street. Here turn right to return to the car park.

A short diversion to the left, however, brings you to a path on the left beside the war memorial, which rises steeply to Caergwrle Castle, a superb viewpoint. The meagre remains are of a late 12th-century castle originally built by Dafydd ap Gruffyd, the brother of Llewellyn ap Gruffyd who was the last independent Prince of Wales. It was later rebuilt by Edward I after his successful Welsh campaigns but abandoned shortly afterwards.

Descend from the castle and walk along High Street back to the start. ●

Criccieth and Llanystumdwy

		GPS waypoints
Start	Criccieth	☑ SH 499 378
Distance	4¾ miles (7.5km)	**Ⓐ** SH 496 376
Height gain	240 feet (75m)	**Ⓑ** SH 477 374
Approximate time	2 hours	**Ⓒ** SH 479 382
Parking	Car park in Criccieth	**Ⓓ** SH 477 386
Route terrain	Moorland; coastal margins; farmland; some road walking	**Ⓔ** SH 483 382
Ordnance Survey maps	Landranger 123 (Lleyn Peninsula), Explorer 254 (Lleyn Peninsula East)	

This is an easy half-day stroll in the flat coastal area of the Lleyn Peninsula between Criccieth and Llanystumdwy. It is very much 'Lloyd George' country: the great Welsh statesman spent much of his life here and the walk passes the Lloyd George Museum, his grave and memorial above the River Dwyfor, and Ty-newydd, the house where he spent his last years. For much of the way there are fine views across to the Rhinogs beyond Harlech.

The small, pleasant resort of Criccieth is dominated by its castle, situated on a headland between two fine beaches and looking across Tremadog Bay to Harlech Castle. It was originally a native Welsh castle, built in the 13th century during the reign of Llywelyn the Great, but after Edward I's conquest of Wales it was taken over and extended by the English king to serve as a part of the ring of powerful fortresses encircling Snowdonia. Owain Glyndwr captured and burned it in 1404 during his uprising, and it appears never to have been garrisoned again, falling into ruin.

🖊 The walk starts by the castle entrance. Head west along the coastal road to reach a triangular green **Ⓐ**. At low tide you can simply drop to the beach and walk along the foreshore to reach point **Ⓑ**. At other times bend right with the road past the **Abereistedd Hotel** and walk uphill until the road narrows, just past a Scout and Guide hall. Here, turn between gateposts along a rough drive for Muriau (not Muriau cul-de-sac). At the fold of cottages, go to the right of the farthest house, Ty Cerrig, joining a gated, grassy bridleway.

At the junction with a gravel lane turn left, shortly go through a gate and walk to the house. Turn right along the track to reach the gateway to another house. Pass to the right of the property along a good path. At the end of the garden, turn left along a fenced path. This sweeps around amid luxuriant vegetation to reach the beach at a National Trust plinth. Walk ahead 100yds to a gate on the right. This is where the return leg comes in, but you should stay on the old lane just above

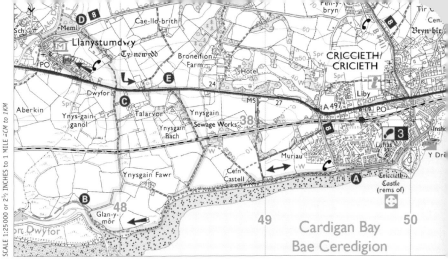

the beach. As this bends right towards a farm complex, fork left along a grassier track, remaining above the curve of the secluded bay. Sublime views ahead stretch down the Lleyn Peninsula's serrated spine, while to the left Harlech Castle is set against the backdrop of the rugged Rhinogs.

Continue upstream beside the tiny estuary of the Afon Dwyfor (to your left). Where this sweeps left **B**, look right for a path between two old huts and walk this between high hedges to an old gate and hand-gate. Go through and turn left along the farm road. This bends several times to reach another gate and stile. Bear left at a T-junction a few paces beyond and keep ahead along a broad, stony track, crossing the railway line and continuing up to the Criccieth–Pwllheli road **C**.

Turn left along the road and take the first turning on the right through the village of Llanystumdwy, passing the Lloyd George Museum on the right and continuing to a bridge.

Just before the bridge turn right along a lane for a few yards, and at a public footpath sign turn left into the riverside woods to Lloyd George's grave and memorial, designed by the renowned Welsh architect Clough Williams-Ellis, best known for his Italian-style village of Portmeirion, not far away on the other side of Tremadog Bay.

Continue along the lane and at a public footpath sign **D** turn right along the drive to Ty-newydd, bearing left in front of the house where Lloyd George spent his last years and in which he died in 1945. Continue, passing a row of single-storeyed cottages on the left, to a kissing-gate, go through, down some steps and turn right to keep along the edge of fields. Climb more steps in a wall and turn left downhill along the left-hand edge of a field, by a hedge on the left, to go through a kissing-gate, on to the main road again.

Turn left along it for ¼ mile and at a public footpath sign **E** turn right down a tree-lined drive. Where the drive bends to the right keep ahead, go up steps and along a path and up more steps at the side of a house. Walk along a grassy path, going through a kissing-gate and passing under a very low railway bridge, to continue along what is now a broad, hedge-lined track down to the sea. Turn left on joining the coast path to retrace your steps to Criccieth, with superb views of the castle perched on its rock in the foreground and the dramatic skyline of Snowdonia on the horizon. ●

Along the River Clywd

		GPS waypoints
Start	Rhyl (Marine Lake)	🖉 SH 996 806
Distance	5½ miles (9km)	Ⓐ SJ 003 805
Height gain	70 feet (20m)	Ⓑ SJ 006 801
Approximate time	2½ hours	Ⓒ SJ 022 780
Parking	Car park at start (Pay and Display)	
Route terrain	Surfaced riverside paths and gravel tracks; a little road walking	
Ordnance Survey maps	Landranger 116 (Denbigh and Colwyn Bay), Explorer 264 (Vale of Clwyd)	

This largely flat and easy walk simply ambles along both sides of the Afon Clwyd between Rhyl and Rhuddlan, taking in the far-reaching views of the Clwydian Hills and the north-eastern summits of Snowdonia. The river flats and marshes are popular with a range of wetland birds, and a pair of binoculars may well enhance your day with a chance sighting of something rare.

🖉 This is a clockwise circuit, starting at a car park near Foryd Bridge, on the edge of the Marine Lake. Leave the car park at the riverside end, and turn left to walk along the top of an embankment, as far as a railway bridge. Here, dip left through trees into the grounds of the Marine Lake, which is encircled by a miniature railway track.

Rhyl has long been a popular holiday resort along the North Wales coast, with every imaginable amusement to keep visitors entertained. The place is largely a Victorian invention, and the marine lake came about when Rhyl Urban District Council transformed a marsh at the mouth of the river, known as the 'Mudlands', into a boating lake. The site began to boom when Albert Barnes constructed a fun fair here (now no more) in 1910, which took pride of place for nearly 60 years. In 1895, Rhyl was an up-and-coming resort seeking to cash in on the Victorian seaside

holidaying vogue. In 1845, Rhyl boasted some fine, smooth sands extending for several miles, and was a favourite resort for sea bathing frequented by numerous visitors for whom three 'respectable' hotels were established. Before 1826, Rhyl consisted only of a few scattered dwellings.

Go forward between the lake and the miniature railway line, and on the far side of the lake follow the railway line as it swings left, until you can leave the marine park by bearing right into a side street. At a crossroads, turn right and walk to, and over, a pedestrian footbridge spanning the main North Wales railway line Ⓐ. Immediately over the bridge, turn right, through a gate giving into Glan Morfa Community Woodland. Here the landscape is in the process of being transformed from a landfill rubbish tip into new woodland, a project started in 2006.

As soon as you pass through the gate,

the ongoing path divides. Branch left and now follow the surfaced path as it loops around the edge of the embryonic woodland to meet an inlet, where it is deflected inland. Continue as far as another path division **B**, and there turn right to cross the inlet (signed for Brickfields Pond).

Press on along the surfaced path, which soon heads back towards the river, and then follows it all the way to Rhuddlan. On the way you pass beneath the modern A525, and a short way further on reach the edge of Rhuddlan **C**.

Of particular note as you reach Rhuddlan is the imposing castle, one of 17 built by Edward I in his campaign to suppress the Welsh. Just beyond the castle is the only remaining part of its

Old Parliament House is said to be where Edward I enacted the Statute of Rhuddlan in 1284, which brought Wales fully under English administration and divided the country into counties on the English pattern.

As you reach the edge of Rhuddlan, turn right across a footbridge spanning the river, and continue beside the main road on the other side, as far as the turning into Marsh Road. Here, turn right, and now simply follow an almost arrow-straight lane and track past the Sun Valley Caravan Park and towards Rhyl, with lovely views across the marsh and its birdlife.

As you approach the railway line again, dip left to use a tunnel beneath it, and then walk out towards Foryd Bridge, beside which **The Harbour** pub is a convenient place for a little refreshment before crossing the road-bridge to complete the walk. ●

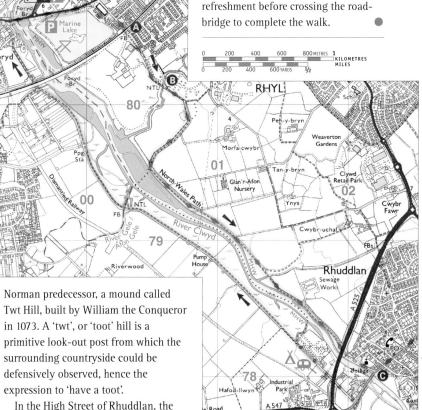

Norman predecessor, a mound called Twt Hill, built by William the Conqueror in 1073. A 'twt', or 'toot' hill is a primitive look-out post from which the surrounding countryside could be defensively observed, hence the expression to 'have a toot'.

In the High Street of Rhuddlan, the

SCALE 1:27777 or 2¼ INCHES to 1 MILE 3.6CM to 1KM

Denbigh and the Ystrad valley

		GPS waypoints
Start	Denbigh	
Distance	5 miles (8km)	✏ SJ 050 661
Height gain	575 feet (175m)	Ⓐ SJ 050 656
		Ⓑ SJ 057 649
Approximate time	2½ hours	Ⓒ SJ 054 649
Parking	Car parks in Denbigh	Ⓓ SJ 044 652
		Ⓔ SJ 032 650
Route terrain	Urban streets; farmland; riverside paths	Ⓕ SJ 049 657
Ordnance Survey maps	Landranger 116 (Denbigh and Colwyn Bay), Explorer 264 (Vale of Clwyd)	

Although a short walk, this route abounds with interest and provides a succession of outstanding views across the Vale of Clwyd. From Denbigh you descend into the valley of the little River Ystrad and follow its course across meadows and through woodland, to the ruins of a small cottage associated with Dr Johnson. Near the end comes a dramatic view of Denbigh Castle, perched on its hill above the town and Vale with the long line of the Clwydian range on the horizon.

The walled town of Denbigh is dominated by the ruins of its late-13th-century castle. It was built by the powerful Henry de Lacy, Earl of Lincoln, who was entrusted by Edward I with the task of keeping the local area firmly under English control. Apart from its extent, the most impressive feature of the castle is the elaborate three-towered gateway. Most of the town walls, contemporary with the castle, survive, though the modern town has moved down the hill outside them. Within the walls are the remains of two churches. The first is the shell of an Elizabethan cathedral, 'Leicester's Church', intended by Robert Dudley, Earl of Leicester and Lord of Denbigh, to replace the cathedral at St Asaph but never completed. The second is a surviving tower from the medieval town chapel of St Hilary.

✏ The walk begins in the town centre, facing the Library and Museum Gallery. Pass to the right of it, turn right steeply up Bull Lane, go round a right bend and continue up St Hilary's Terrace, passing Leicester's Church. Turn right, then left, passing the tower of St Hilary's Church, and then right again in front of the castle. At a T-junction, turn left below the castle walls, head down to another T-junction Ⓐ and turn left.

At a public footpath sign turn left along an enclosed track, which later narrows to a hedge-lined path. The path descends, but before reaching the bottom, turn right at a footpath sign and walk along the fenced path to use a kissing-gate. From here head half-left,

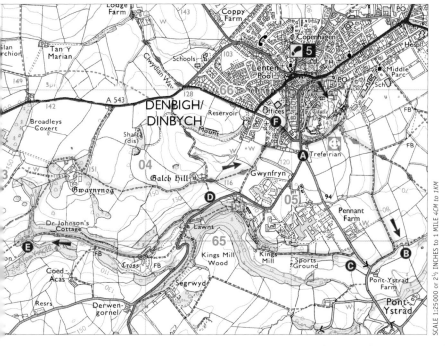

SCALE 1:25000 or 2½ INCHES to 1 MILE 4CM to 1KM

| 0 | 200 | 400 | 600 | 800 METRES | 1 |
| 0 | 200 | 400 | 600 YARDS | ½ | |

KILOMETRES
MILES

gently downhill across the sloping pasture to the bottom corner and a stile and kissing-gate. Use the stile, put the hedge on your left and walk to and through another kissing-gate; keep the hedge left to reach several gateways at a corner. Go straight on, putting a hedge on your right, and walk on to a stile. Climb this and hug the top of the field to another stile in a corner **B**.

Climb this stile and walk along the wooded path, an occasionally very narrow passage. Climb two stiles before eventually reaching a lane. Turn right, uphill and walk to find a finger-posted track **C** on your left beside a copse.

Turn along this and remain on it, eventually passing in front of a remote house. Beyond here the track shrinks to a wide woodland path, shortly passing through a hand-gate. Remain on this peaceful path just above the River Ystrad to reach an old gate blocking the

way. Fork left here, climb the nearby stile and walk the left side of the riverside meadow. Climb another stile and keep ahead, joining the green hollow to the right of a distinct mound. Go through a field gate and ahead past the cottage to a corner stile. Climb this and turn right up the lane.

In 200yds, double back to the left along a grassy, hedged track **D**. This passes behind a range of estate buildings before becoming a wooded path. Continue on this path, crossing two stile/gates before entering a riverside meadow – on your right is the tree-shrouded ruin of Dr Johnson's Cottage, said to be where the renowned traveller and lexicographer stayed during a tour of Wales. At the end of the meadow go through a kissing-gate into woodland, and immediately fork right up a steep path **E** to the top edge of the trees.

Climb the stile and turn right up beside the woods; the field funnels into a long entry and another stile. Climb this and bend left (ignore the stile into

Denbigh and Denbigh Castle

more woods) on a field track beside a small quarry area that leads to a gateway. Go through this and walk ahead to a stone and slate stile at a wooded corner. Take this and keep right to a farther kissing-gate; once through this, bend right along the edge of the large field outside the estate wall. Use another kissing-gate beside a gate on your right and keep ahead along a dirt road. Cross straight over the driveway to the imposing Gwaynynog Manor (where Beatrix Potter worked on illustrations for her books) and walk on with the field road, grand views of the Clwydian range drawing the eye ahead.

Pass through another kissing-gate and head a hair's breadth left, aiming for a stile beneath an oak in the far field boundary. From here are excellent views across to Denbigh Castle. Walk along the left side of the field (ignore the stile in 20 paces) to use another stile in 100yds. Keep to the left of this field to drop to a gate on the left past a cottage. Through this, turn right joining a rough lane. Walk this lane to a finger-posted stone stile on your left. Climb this and walk diagonally right to the far corner and a stone stile beside a gateway (Clwydian Way marker). Use this and trace the right side of the field to take a kissing-gate into an enclosed path behind housing.

This bends left to emerge on an estate road. Turn left to reach a T-junction **F**. Turn right and immediately cross the road to join a tarred path on the left dropping past allotment gardens. Keep ahead on the lane at the bottom to reach a junction. Turn right to return to the centre of Denbigh. ●

A taste of the Llangollen Canal

		GPS waypoints
Start	Llangollen	📸 SJ 217 421
Distance	4½ miles (7km)	Finish, at Trevor, SJ 271 422
Height gain	260 feet (80m)	
Approximate time	2½ hours	
Parking	Car park in village	
Route terrain	Clear tracks, woodland paths	
Ordnance Survey maps	Landranger 117 (Chester and Wrexham), Explorer 255 (Llangollen & Berwyn)	

As might be expected, a walk that is almost entirely alongside a canal is not going to need much in the way of route description; and this is certainly the case with this delightful amble from the centre of Llangollen to the village of Pontcysyllte, renowned for its remarkable aqueduct. The walk is necessarily linear, but if the day is especially pleasant, there is no finer return to Llangollen than to walk back along the canal, from any point in the walk. Traveline Cymru (www.traveline-cymru.info. Tel: 08712 002233) details bus services that operate between Trevor, just north of the walk's end at Pontcysyllte, and Llangollen.

Linking Llangollen in Denbighshire with Hurleston in South Cheshire, the Llangollen Canal is a navigable canal, crossing the border between England and Wales. In 2009, 11 miles of the canal, from Gledrid Bridge, near Rhoswiel, to the Horseshoe Falls, which includes Chirk Aqueduct and Pontcysyllte Aqueduct, was declared a World Heritage site.

The waterway was built when work to complete the Ellesmere Canal was halted in the early 19th century. The Ellesmere Canal was intended to be a commercial waterway linking the Port of Liverpool to the West Midlands. Beset with problems, however, the scheme was never completed. As the waterway

never reached its proposed main source of water at Moss Valley, Wrexham, a feeder channel was constructed along the side of the Vale of Llangollen to the River Dee: this work created the Horseshoe Falls at Llantysilio.

📸 Leave the long stay car park in Llangollen, and walk briefly alongside the River Dee towards the town centre, before ascending steps to the road, near the **Bridge End Hotel**. Cross the road with care, and take the first turning on the right, just before the hotel, and on reaching Minffordd, swing to the left, ascending, to reach the canal towpath (seasonal **tea room** nearby). On reaching the canal, turn right beneath Bridge 45W to set off along the towpath.

Initially, the canal is high above the A539, as it ambles easily along with improving vistas off to the left of Castell Dinas Bran (see Walk 26) and the limestone escarpment of Trevor Rocks putting on a fine display. Continue under Bridge 43W and pass an isolated cottage. Soon, the canal passes beneath the A-road, and continues its way. Bridge 41W gives access to a hotel called **Sun Trevor**, which serves a range of fine ales and beers and serves food.

Now, with agreeable views ahead and to the south, the canal eases onward, once more switching sides at Bridge 32W. When the towpath emerges onto a road, near Pen-y-bont, cross diagonally left through the basin of Anglo-Welsh Waterway Holidays. Cross the bridge ahead, and turn right to walk to the edge of the famous Pontcysyllte Aqueduct. The aqueduct and canal are early and outstanding examples of innovation inspired by the Industrial Revolution, where they made decisive development in transport capacities possible. It is for this reason that they were accorded World Heritage status. ●

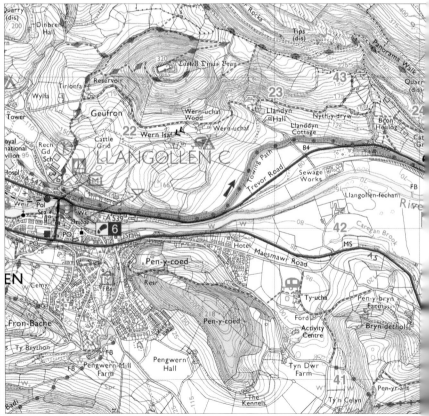

Striding out along the Llangollen Canal

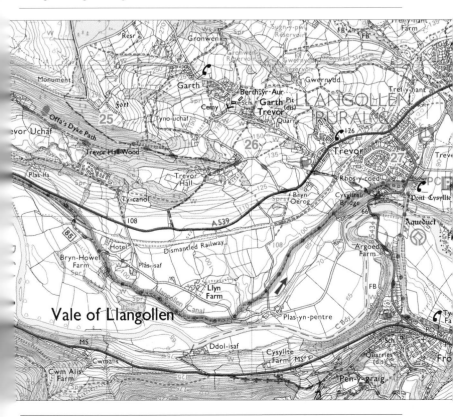

Around Aber

		GPS waypoints
Start	Bont Newydd, Aber	✐ SH 662 720
Distance	4 miles (6.5km)	Ⓐ SH 668 701
Height gain	1,175 feet (360m)	Ⓑ SH 662 700
Approximate time	2½ hours	Ⓒ SH 661 705
Parking	Car park at start (Pay and Display). If this is full, cross the bridge and turn right to the upper car park	Ⓓ SH 660 717
		Ⓔ SH 654 722
Route terrain	Broad woodland tracks, rough moorland, farmland	
Ordnance Survey maps	Landranger 115 (Snowdon/Yr Wyddfa), Explorer OL17 (Snowdon/Yr Wyddfa)	

The walk to Aber Falls (Rhaeadr-fawr) is popular at any time of year, a simple, straightforward trek to one of Nature's most magnificent spectacles. This walk continues the journey, and loops westward along the North Wales Path to the base of the less well-known falls, Rhaeadr-bach, before changing direction again and striking northwards across the base of Moel Wnion, and finishing with a steep flourish that plunges back down to the Aber road.

✐ Begin by passing through the nearby gate, walking upstream into Coedydd Aber National Nature Reserve. A rising path climbs above the Afon Rhaeadr-fawr before dropping to cross a footbridge and leading out to a gate giving onto a broad track: this point is reached directly from the upper car park.

Turn right and simply follow the broad trail, initially rising gently, and then running forward easily as the Aber Falls come into view.

The valley provides a varied range of habitats, from mixed woodland to grassland, and hosts many features of historic and archaeological interest, including an Iron Age hill fort and the remains of several round houses. There are the remains of a roundhouse and a drying kiln on the right, on the approach to the falls, thought to date from the Iron Age, beside which a standing stone is probably much older.

On approaching the spectacular falls, go through a gate, and pass above a footbridge to a splendid viewing point directly below the falls. Return to cross the footbridge Ⓐ, and climb steps on the other side. From the top of the steps, walk forward to a gate on the right.

Beyond the gate, step carefully along a rocky path and eventually drop to another footbridge at the base of Rhaeadr-bach, not quite as impressive as the main falls, but a fine display nonetheless. A short way farther on, the route swings to the right, as a broad green track Ⓑ. This leads to a stream crossing on stepping stones from where the route continues to follow a broad

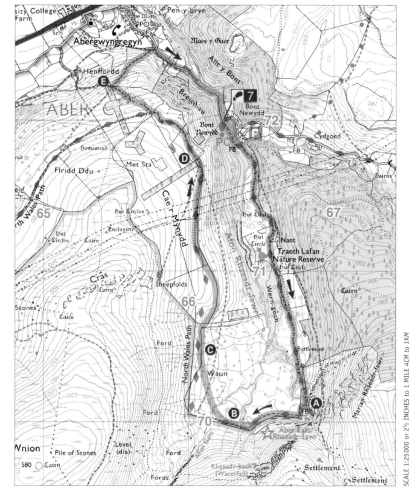

SCALE 1:25000 or 2½ INCHES to 1 MILE 4CM to 1KM

trail that undulates across the hill slope.

Keep on to reach a waymark **C**, and here drop below the green track for a while, rejoining it a short way farther on, and swinging through an S-bend to reach a gate. Beyond, the green track now ascends, and then passes below powerlines. Keep on, to pass through another gate **D**, now with Puffin Island and the tip of Anglesey in view ahead. Walk along the track to the first of two gates close together, between which stands another waymark post. Pass through the first gate, and then almost

immediately descend to the right (north-west), here leaving the North Wales Path, which has accompanied the walk from Bont Newydd.

Continue descending to a point directly below a single gate in a fence up on the left **E**. Here, leave the main track, and branch right onto a narrow trod below a line of old fence posts, descending steeply across the grain of the hill slope. The path is tricky, loose in places and can be slippery. The route passes through an intermediate gate, before slipping down to a final gate that gives onto the Aber village road. Now turn right and walk the road back to the Bont Newydd car park. ●

Penmaenmawr and the Druid's Circle

		GPS waypoints
Start	Penmaenmawr, by the library in town centre	✎ SH 719 762
Distance	4½ miles (7.2km)	**Ⓐ** SH 721 759
Height gain	1,170 feet (355m)	**Ⓑ** SH 721 747
Approximate time	2½ hours	**Ⓒ** SH 720 746
Parking	Car park at start	**Ⓓ** SH 730 759
Route terrain	Farmland and rough hill slopes	**Ⓔ** SH 727 758
Ordnance Survey maps	Landranger 115 (Snowdon/Yr Wyddfa), Explorer OL17 (Snowdon/Yr Wyddfa)	**Ⓕ** SH 725 756

Because the initial climb from Penmaenmawr is steep and unrelenting, it's best to take your time in order to enjoy the grand views over the mountains, the coast and Anglesey. The route leads onto open moorland on the slopes of the eastern Carneddau and passes a druid's circle, the most outstanding and atmospheric of the many prehistoric remains in the area. After a fresh and invigorating ramble across the moorland, there is a relatively easy descent back to the town.

The small coastal town of Penmaenmawr is squeezed between mountains and sea and hemmed in by steep headlands on either side. Before the 19th century, it was largely cut off by land, as travellers had to go over the top of the headlands – a hazardous journey – but the Victorians quarried away part of Penmaen Mawr and tunnelled a railway and road through between Conwy and Bangor. During this time, it became a popular seaside resort, much favoured by Gladstone, and has a fine sandy beach. But its heyday ended with changing tastes and the growth of foreign travel.

✎ Turn right out of the car park and immediately right again along Y Berllan. Take the first turning on the left – almost doubling back – then the next turning on the right and, where the road ends, keep ahead along an enclosed, hedge-lined track, the left-hand one of two beyond the road name plaque for Y Berllan. Head gently uphill to join Craiglwyd Road **Ⓐ**, turn right and at a public footpath sign to the Druid's Circle, turn left up a farm track.

Climb a ladder-stile, pass to the left of the farm and at a wall corner, bear right and head up a grassy bank to go through a metal kissing-gate. Now comes the start of the steep and quite tiring climb onto the moorland above Penmaenmawr. After a few yards bear left and keep left to follow a clear, grassy, uphill path through bracken. The benches that once offered rest stops for the thousands of visitors for whom Penmaenmawr was a popular

Along the way at Foel Lus

destination are now ruinous, although some have been replaced, but the splendid bluebell woods remain, as do the superb views across the bay to the Great Orme. The path later bears to the right, becomes steeper and eventually turns left, crosses a concrete section laid over wet and boggy ground and continues up to a metal gate.

From here there is a particularly fine view of Penmaenmawr below, cradled between the steep headlands of Penmaen Mawr (from which the town gets its name) and Penmaen Bach.

Go through the gate, turn right and follow the wall to a small stone enclosure **Ⓑ**, then turn left onto a track which is part of the North Wales Path (NWP), itself part of the Wales Coast Path inaugurated in 2012. The wide, grassy track passes by an NWP waymark post and rises gradually along the moorland edge. Back to your left are the fringes of the imposing Graiglwyd

granite quarries, stone from which was used to cobble the streets of Lancashire's industrial towns and cities. Much earlier, Neolithic craftsmen made stone axes here. Products of this 'Graig Llwyd Axe Factory' were traded across the rest of Britain and Europe. In the background is Puffin Island, off the eastern tip of Anglesey. On reaching a second NWP waymark at a distinct left-hand kink in the track, divert sharply back right along a grassy path that climbs directly to the stones breaking the horizon

The stones are those of Maeni Hirion, the Druid's Circle **Ⓒ**, although they stretch farther back into the mists of time than the druids, dating back to the Bronze Age, perhaps 4,000 years ago. There's a smaller stone circle beyond, and the moors of these northern fringes of the Carneddau range are liberally littered with standing stones, cists and burials.

Retrace your steps to the North Wales Path and continue eastwards, soon picking up the line of a wall on your right. Follow the direction of a footpath post to the right, go through a metal kissing-gate, keep ahead and at the next footpath post, turn left along a beautiful tree-lined track, passing to the right of a house. In the field on the right is a standing stone.

Keep ahead along the track, going through a metal gate. Continue ahead, ignoring a metal gate and North Wales Path sign off to the right. Go through another metal gate, eventually bearing left to join a track which starts to descend. Turn sharp left in front of gateposts **D** to continue more steeply downhill on a tarmac track. Go over a cattle-grid and, ignoring a footpath sign, continue ahead as far as the next public footpath sign on the left **E**.

Climb steps on your left here opposite a covered reservoir, go through a metal kissing-gate and trace the right-hand edge of sheep pasture, passing above a large old country house. Keep ahead along a wider field-edge track bounded by a line of tall trees. Look for a kissing-gate and low ladder-stile on your right halfway along this strand of trees, climb it and bear left alongside the fence above a trout fishery **F**. Bend right and remain on the enclosed path between the fishery and a caravan park. At the bottom take a kissing-gate beside a metal gate and turn left to descend the tarred drive. Upon reaching the T-junction with a lane, turn left and then immediately right into an enclosed path **A**, here rejoining the outward leg of the walk. Simply retrace this initial stretch back to the start. ●

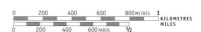

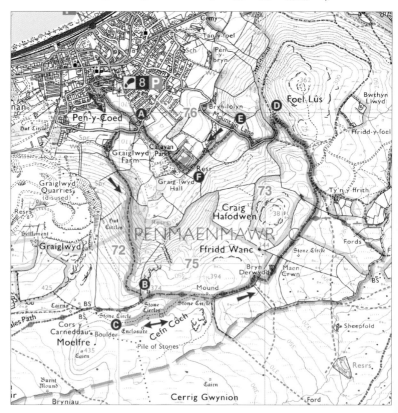

Heathery mountain slopes above Llyn Dinas

Ty Mawr and the Pontcysyllte Aqueduct

Ty Mawr and the Pontcysyllte Aqueduct

		GPS waypoints
Start	Ty Mawr Country Park	☑ SJ 283 414
Distance	5½ miles (9km).	Ⓐ SJ 270 420
	Shorter version: 3 miles (4.8km)	Ⓑ SJ 268 421
Height gain	500 feet (150m)	Ⓒ SJ 259 423
Approximate time	3 hours	Ⓓ SJ 251 419
Parking	Ty Mawr Country Park	Ⓔ SJ 249 417
Route terrain	Farmland, riverside walking and	Ⓕ SJ 268 421
	canal towpath	
Ordnance Survey maps	Landranger 117 (Chester & Wrexham),	
	Explorer 256 (Wrexham & Llangollen)	

There is pleasant waterside walking to be had on this route, beside the River Dee as well as along the towpath of the Llangollen branch of the Shropshire Union Canal. But the most impressive feature of the route is the towering and dramatic Pontcysyllte Aqueduct, which carries the canal over the Dee valley. The walk climbs beside the aqueduct, but the shorter version omits most of the canalside walking.

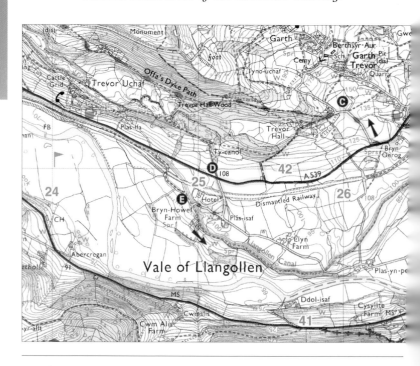

Ty Mawr Country Park has excellent facilities for families, including tame animals and a variety of farm stock, and is an ideal place to start this largely level walk in the valley of the river Dee.

📷 Put your back to the Visitor Centre entrance and turn left, walk along the right-edge of the tarred play area through a kissing-gate beside a gate at the far end. Turn right and go through a gate in a fence – there's a fingerpost here 'Country Park Walk and Aqueduct.' The surfaced path gradually descends and bends left, passing by donkey, goat and sheep enclosures.

Soon after the path levels out, turn right through a gate signed 'Footpath to Aqueduct'. Drop down the steps and follow the boardwalk through a copse to reach riverside meadows. The surfaced path skirts these above the Dee, with views ahead (when the trees are not in leaf) to the aqueduct. Beyond the wide concrete bridge, pass to the right of the pumping station and trace the path through to a point beneath Pontcysyllte Aqueduct. This was designed by the renowned canal engineers Thomas Telford and William Jessop and opened in 1805, carrying the Llangollen branch of the Shropshire Union Canal at a height of 127ft (38m) above the River Dee. At over 1000ft (305m) in length it is one of the true engineering marvels of the Industrial Revolution, a giant technological leap for the time.

Look for the steps on the right **Ⓐ** immediately before the aqueduct and ascend these, pass under the last arch and walk up to a road. Turn right, cross a bridge over the canal by Trevor Basin and turn left on to the towpath, here joining Offa's Dyke Path. Turn left over the first footbridge and continue along the other bank of the canal.

At an Offa's Dyke Path fingerpost **Ⓕ** turn left for the shorter walk, picking up route directions from the next point at which **Ⓕ** appears in the text.

For the full walk turn right over the

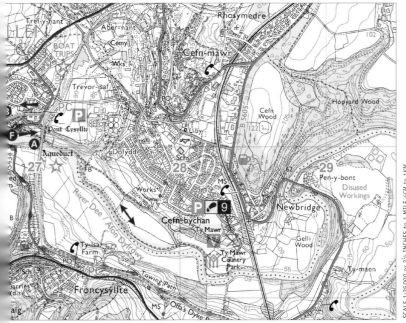

SCALE 1:25000 or 2½ INCHES to 1 MILE 4CM to 1KM

next footbridge **B** bear left and head diagonally across a field to a kissing-gate. Climb it, turn left to walk below the embankment of a disused railway and the path bends right to pass through a tunnel. Turn right, follow the path to the left and continue along an enclosed tarmac path, climbing steps to a road. Turn left, cross the road and walk the pavement to reach, on your right, Trevor Hall Road. Turn along this and trace the quiet lane to a right-hand bend **C**. Here, fork left along the gravelled drive, signed as Offa's Dyke Path. Keep ahead on this as Offa's Dyke Path departs to the right; in the trees to your left is the little 18th century estate church.

Just before reaching Trevor Hall, turn left and climb a stile next to a field gate, then bear right down the descending track beside a fence on your left. Pass below the woods and bend left to a stile, then a second one and a third near a house, and walk ahead to the road. Turn right on the narrow pavement.

In 300 yds turn left along the lane **D** signed for **Bryn Howel Hotel**. Walk past the hotel driveway and on to a junction. Turn right along the roughening lane (there's a 'Low Bridge' restriction sign here) and walk to and across the canal bridge **E**.

Circle back-right underneath this bridge, putting the canal on your left and joining the tranquil, tree-lined towpath. There are pleasant views of the River Dee below and the surrounding hills, and later Pontcysyllte Aqueduct comes into sight again. At a metal bridge (No. 33) you briefly rejoin the outward route but at an Offa's Dyke Path fingerpost **F** bear right off the towpath and drop down the path to a driveway. Look half-right for a way-marked flight of steps leading down to a road. For a great view of the aqueduct and River Dee divert right down to a bridge (200yds); otherwise turn left uphill and walk to the left-hand bend where a fingerpost directs you right, back onto the outward leg of the walk and the steps down beside the aqueduct. Simply retrace the route back to Ty Mawr Country Park, with the graceful railway viaduct as a background. ●

Boat on Pontcysyllte Aqueduct

Chirk and the River Ceiriog

		GPS waypoints	
Start	Chirk	☑	SJ 291 376
Distance	5¾ miles (9.2km)	Ⓐ	SJ 283 377
Height gain	975 feet (295m)	Ⓑ	SJ 281 378
Approximate time	3 hours	Ⓒ	SJ 263 389
Parking	Car park near start	Ⓓ	SJ 264 374
Route terrain	Parkland, farmland and meadows	Ⓔ	SJ 267 370
		Ⓕ	SJ 280 371
Ordnance Survey maps	Landranger 126 (Shrewsbury & Oswestry), Explorer 240 (Oswestry) and 256 (Wrexham & Llangollen)	Ⓖ	SJ 290 372

After an attractive walk across the parkland surrounding Chirk Castle, with fine views of the great border fortress, the route joins the Offa's Dyke Path and drops into the lovely Ceiriog valley. It then climbs, and continues along the south side of the valley before descending again to the river. The final stretch keeps by the Ceiriog, crossing delightful meadows and passing beneath the adjacent 19th-century viaduct and the 18th-century aqueduct, built to carry different forms of transport across the valley and both engineering triumphs of their respective eras.

Note that this route can only be walked between 1 April and 30 September as part of it, between Ⓑ and Ⓒ, uses a National Trust permissive path which is open only between those dates.

📝 Start at the crossroads in village centre by the medieval church and turn along Church Street. Take the first turning on the left, by the war memorial, keep ahead over first a railway bridge, and then over the canal, and turn right Ⓐ at a public footpath sign. Follow the path ahead through the woods, keeping to the left-hand path and looking for a wooden hand-gate down to the left in 200yds. Use this and walk up the sloping field to another hand-gate into a lane.

Cross into the entry Ⓑ virtually opposite and take a hand-gate beside a field gate. *This is the start of the permissive path through Chirk Park, open only between 1 April and 30 September. It is well marked by large, white-tipped posts.* Keep to the left edge of the field to use another hand-gate beside a field gate, from which head half-right across the parkland to use a hand-gate through a fence. Turn left, shortly use another hand-gate (not the one on your left) and soon join the line of the inner state wall on your left. Drift right to find a stile onto the main castle drive at a T-Junction. Go ahead along the road towards the car park.

On this part of the walk there are impressive views of Chirk Castle, completed in 1310, but regularly altered and modernised over the centuries.

Unlike most of the other border fortresses, it has been continuously occupied since it was built, mostly by the Myddleton family. It is now a National Trust property and its elegant state rooms and formal gardens are well worth a visit.

Keep right at the fork into the car park. Stay alongside the left edge of the car park to the very end at a cattle-grid, here taking the first of a series of hand-gates beside field gates, all marked by white-tipped posts. Simply remain along the left edge of the pastures to reach a tarred lane at a bend.

Immediately past the lodge house 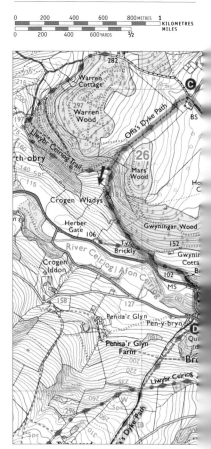 on your left, turn left through a kissing-gate, joining the Offa's Dyke Path (marked by an acorn logo). Trace the field road to and past a redundant stile and ahead to a ridge-top kissing-gate. Continue ahead along the right edge of the woodland to a stile beside a metal gate. Beyond this the path steepens, dropping to a kissing-gate into a rough lane. All the while there are fine views down into the Ceiriog valley. Turn left down this lane, which becomes tarred at a farm. Remain on it to reach a junction above some cottages. Here turn left and trace the lane all the way to the main road. Take the lane opposite (entering Shropshire here), cross the bridge over the River Ceiriog and rise steeply to a T-junction.

Turn left **D** and remain on the lane for about ½ mile to a left-bend immediately past an old school **E**. Turn left here down the old lane marked by multiple waymark discs. This gives out between a cottage and a barn; keep ahead here through two close-spaced gates and along the grassy path to a kissing-gate. Through it bear right to reach a stile into the Woodland Trust's Pentre Wood. Climb this and join the path; in 150yds climb the flight of steps

on your right, then remain on the path as it soon drops back down more steps and comes close to the River Ceiriog, eventually to leave the woods and enter a meadow. Stick with the path close to the riverside trees; this eventually becomes a wider track and rises to a stile beside a gate at the foot of a rake of cottages. Turn left to a T-junction and left again to cross Pont-faen bridge.

Turn right through a kissing-gate **F** into the field immediately beyond the bridge and pick up the path that roughly follows the riverbank. Ahead, two multi-arched structures march across the valley. The nearest is a 19th-century railway viaduct; the farthest is Thomas Telford's aqueduct carrying the Llangollen branch of the

The viaduct and aqueduct at Chirk

Shropshire Union Canal across the valley, impressive but not as amazing as his Pontcysyllte Aqueduct across the River Dee just a couple of miles away (see Walk 9). Use the kissing-gate and hand-gate beneath the structures and walk ahead, shortly bending left up a fenced track to find a gate onto the road near Chirk Bridge **G**. Cross over, bear slightly left through a metal gate, at a public footpath sign, and walk along a track. Where it curves to the right, keep ahead along an enclosed path, climb a stile, turn right over a ditch and then turn left alongside it. Bear right to head uphill along a grassy path, climb a stile, and turn right along a road to return to the start.

●

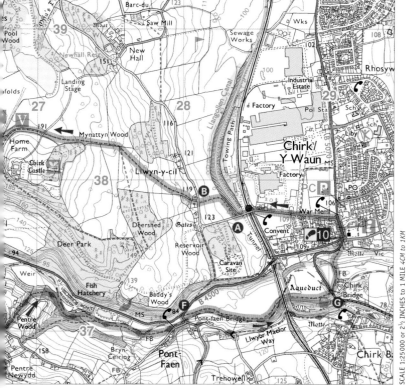

Prestatyn Hillside

		GPS waypoints
Start	Prestatyn Hillside Viewpoint car park, ½ mile north of Gwaenysgor	🏁 SJ 074 819
Distance	5¼ miles (8.3km)	Ⓐ SJ 075 810
Height gain	760 feet (230m)	Ⓑ SJ 072 805
Approximate time	3 hours	Ⓒ SJ 062 800
Parking	Car park at start	Ⓓ SJ 062 794
Route terrain	Hill road walking and farmland pastures	Ⓔ SJ 065 809
		Ⓕ SJ 070 813
Ordnance Survey maps	Landranger 116 (Denbigh & Colwyn Bay), Explorers 264 (Vale of Clwyd) and 265 (Clwydian Range)	

On this walk in the most northerly part of the Carneddau, there are extensive views over Prestatyn (which lies immediately below), Rhyl, the Vale of Clwyd and the North Wales coast. Most of the second half of the route uses first a disused railway track, and later a stretch of Offa's Dyke Path as it climbs above Bishopswood, which clothes the steep hillside.

🏁 Start by turning right out of the car park and walking along the lane into the quiet village of Gwaenysgor. Just past the church and a children's play area Ⓐ, turn right along a lane and a few yards after the lane becomes a rough track, take the finger-posted stone stile on the left immediately after the driveway for 'Tir Gwelyog', entering a wide grassy track.

Climb a wooden stile and then, at a bend, take the gate-side stone stile in the corner and turn right along the field edge to find another stile in a corner. Climb this and look half-left to sight a cottage. Aim for this climbing a stile and head for the field corner near the cottage, where a stile gives access to a lane Ⓑ. Turn right and remain on this lane for ¾ mile.

Good views open out across the Vale of Clwyd and the prominent hill of Graig Fawr on your right. Keep left at a junction, remaining on the lane to reach another junction just before a National Trust car park Ⓒ. Here turn left along another lane and after 300yds, turn right over a stile. Walk across a field, climb a stile and keep along the top edge of a sloping field, heading gently downhill. At the bottom turn left along a rough track and shortly fork right along a wider track. In 50yds, look on your right for a small wooden bridge leading to a metal kissing-gate, take this and walk through a belt of trees to the edge of a meadow. Bear half-right to find a kissing-gate in the corner. Use this and turn left with the finger-post for the Prestatyn–Dyserth Way, descending a flight of wooden steps to gain the tarred trackbed of a former railway Ⓓ.

Turn right along this and go under the bridge. This was the old London and North Western Railway branch line

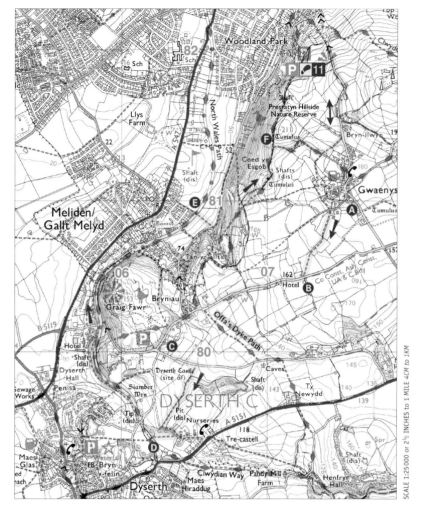

```
0      200    400    600    800 METRES   1
                                         KILOMETRES
                                         MILES
0      200    400    600 YARDS            ½
```

from Prestatyn to Dyserth, and you remain on it for the next 1¼ miles. Pass by the former goods shed at Meliden Station and stay on the track to reach the end of housing on your left (there's also a golf tee here) **E**. Turn left, use the kissing-gate and rise up the steep pasture to another kissing-gate; beyond this walk up the steep tarred lane. This becomes a wooded track, passes through a kissing-gate and in a further 100yds meets a junction with Offa's Dyke Path (ODP). Turn left; in a further

100yds turn left again with the fingerpost for Prestatyn Hillside and ODP, climbing gently through Bishopswood (Coed yr Esgob), once owned by the bishops of St Asaph.

The path becomes fenced above an old quarry then rises to a three-way fingerpost, here bear right on ODP, pass through a wall gap and then rise increasingly steeply through gorse and scrub. The path levels, offering superb views off to your left to the distant horizon of Snowdonia's peaks, and then descends to pass right of a fenced mine-shaft before rising again through a thicket. Emerging from this, you'll soon reach an old fingerpost and a stile on your right **F**. Climb the stile (marked as Gwaenysgor) and walk ahead along the foot of the slope towards the distant village. The path enters low woodland before reaching a kissing-gate, beyond which trace the hedged path to a walled old village well on your right. On your left here, climb the few steps, use the stile and walk ahead to another one, then stick to the right-hand side of the pasture to reach a stile into a lane. Turn left to return to the car park. ●

Graig Fawr cutting, Meliden

Llyn Padarn

		GPS waypoints
Start	Llanberis, village car park beside Llyn Padarn	SH 577 604
Distance	5½ miles (8.9km)	**Ⓐ** SII 575 607
Height gain	960 feet (295m)	**Ⓑ** SH 559 623
Approximate time	3 hours	**Ⓒ** SH 575 617
Parking	Car park at start	**Ⓓ** SH 586 604
Route terrain	Disused railway trackbed, woodland, quarry tracks	**Ⓔ** SH 585 601
Ordnance Survey maps	Landranger 115 (Snowdon/Yr Wyddfa), Explorer OL17 (Snowdon/Yr Wyddfa)	

Llyn Padarn is situated at the foot of Snowdon and this straightforward circuit of the lake, which uses a combination of a disused railway track, lane, woodland and lakeside paths and old quarry tracks, provides, for relatively little effort, a series of memorable views of the surrounding mountains, including spectacular ones of Snowdon itself. As well as pleasant walking beside the lake, there is attractive woodland on the slopes above its eastern side, interesting remains of the slate-quarrying industry that once dominated this part of Snowdonia, and a brief detour to the ruins of Dolbadarn Castle that occupy a commanding position between Llyn Padarn and the adjacent Llyn Peris.

Its splendid situation below Snowdon and between two lakes has enabled the former slate-quarrying village of Llanberis to become a major tourist resort and walking centre. It is the starting point for ascents of Snowdon, both on foot and by the Snowdon Mountain Railway. There is another railway line that runs along the shore of Llyn Padarn, and the many physical remains of the once great slate-quarrying industry only add to its appeal and interest.

Start by walking down to the lake and turn left onto a path that curves left to the road. Turn right and take the first turning on the right Ⓐ to continue along a broad tarmac drive,

the bed of a former railway. After passing a barrier, the drive becomes a rough, tree-lined track (Lon Las Peris) beside Llyn Padarn. Walk through a short tunnel and keep ahead on the fenced path to reach the main road. Cross this, turn right along the verge and climb the ladder-stile about 70yds away on the left. This puts you on the line of the abandoned A4086 road. Pass by a superfluous ladder-stile and remain on the old tarred road, climb a second stile and continue to a nearby road junction beside a cottage. Fork right here to cross an old bridge at the foot of Llyn Padarn. From here there is a magnificent view looking down the

Looking towards Snowdon from Llyn Padarn

an arch and pass below the former workings of Vivian Quarry with a pool below. The quarry was named after W.W. Vivian, who was manager of the Dinorwic Quarry Company at the end of the 19th century.

Just before the lane curves right to pass under a bridge, take the walled path on the right and walk a few paces to cross the steep rail-tracks of an old quarry incline. Turn down beside these, descending to the car park here at the heart of the Welsh Slate Museum complex.

length of the lake towards the Llanberis Pass, with the summit of Snowdon clearly visible.

Turn right along a narrow lane **B**, signposted to Fachwen, which climbs steadily through woodland above the lake and after one mile – just after passing a telephone box – turn right at a public footpath sign **C**, through a metal gate on to a path that descends through trees. This soon joins a tarred lane; walk down this as it gradually winds through lovely woodland, passing remote cottages and roughening as it passes beneath an old quarry bridge. Narrowing, it eventually reaches a footbridge across a tumbling stream. Cross it, turn right, then turn left through a kissing-gate and head steadily uphill, via steps in places, to a superb viewpoint overlooking the lake.

Now the path descends again, at a fork take the right-hand, lower, slabbed path, pass through a wall-gap and continue across a terrace in front of the Quarry Hospital, now a visitor centre, but formerly the hospital for employees of the Dinorwic Quarry Company. Head downhill along a tarmac track, go under

There are myriad attractions here. The main body of the museum is housed in the former workshops of the Dinorwic Quarry Company and contains much of the original machinery, including a large water-wheel. At their height in the Victorian era, when demand for Welsh slate was at its greatest, the Dinorwic quarries were the largest anywhere in the world and employed over 3,000 men. The Llanberis Lake Railway, the terminus of which is next to the museum, was constructed to carry the slate to the docks at Port Dinorwic on the Menai Strait. The quarries closed down in 1969.

To continue the walk from the complex, join the access road **D** with the fenced railway on your left and the main museum buildings to your right. Walk along this and through a wrought-iron gate to a T-junction with another road. Here turn right, immediately crossing a bridge across the spillway (note the retractable barriers) linking the twin lakes Llyn Peris and Llyn Padarn. Off to your left here is the entrance to 'Electric Mountain', a vast underground hydroelectric power station created in the bowels of the former Dinorwig Slate Quarries; it's also a very popular visitor attraction.

In a further 300yds turn left down steps, cross a footbridge over a stream, go through a metal gate and follow a path up steps to Dolbadarn Castle, whose circular keep, situated on a rocky knoll above the lake, still guards the southern end of the Llanberis Pass. It is a native Welsh castle, built by Llewellyn the Great in the early 13th century.

Retrace your steps to the road and cross into the car park opposite. At the far-left corner a kissing-gate leads onto a surfaced path. Turn right along this and wind with it to pass beneath a bridge carrying the Llanberis Lake Railway. In a few paces **E** go straight over the wider path (do not cross the footbridge on your right) to join a grassy path that passes to the left of a slate hut and then strikes across rough meadows here at the head of Llyn Padarn. A few old kissing-gates and flat bridges lead to a footbridge beside an adventure playground, beyond which follow the well-used path beside the lake and through to the village car park. ●

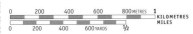

Yr Eifl

		GPS waypoints
Start	Forestry Commission car park ½ mile north of Llithfaen. In Llithfaen take the narrow, uphill road opposite the PO Stores, signed for Nant Gwrtheyrn	📝 SH 353 440 Ⓐ SH 362 454 Ⓑ SH 365 447 Ⓒ SH 374 447 Ⓓ SH 359 437
Distance	3¾ miles (6km)	
Height gain	1,180 feet (360m)	
Approximate time	3 hours	
Parking	Car park at start	
Route terrain	Mountain moorland	
Ordnance Survey maps	Landranger 123 (Lleyn Peninsula), Explorer 254 (Lleyn Peninsula East)	

Despite the fact that only a modest height of 1,850ft (564m) is reached, this is quite a strenuous walk with a fair amount of climbing across terrain similar to that in the higher mountains of Snowdonia. Yr Eifl means 'the Forks' and comprises three neighbouring peaks that rise above the north coast of the Lleyn Peninsula, prominent landmarks visible for many miles. From them the views the length of Lleyn, across the water to Anglesey and along the western edge of Snowdonia are superb.
Do not attempt this walk in misty conditions as route-finding between the summits would be made very difficult.

📝 From the car park turn right along the lane for a short distance and at a bridleway sign turn sharp left onto a broad track which heads steadily uphill to a pass (Bwlch yr Eifl) between the western and central peaks of Yr Eifl. At the top of the pass Ⓐ, a grand view unfolds ahead along the Lleyn coast, with Anglesey and the mountains of Snowdonia on the horizon. At this point, opposite a gate and a track leading up to a transmitting station on the western peak, turn right on to a clear path that heads steadily uphill to the central one of the three peaks, which at 1,850ft (564m) is also the highest. The path winds upwards

between heather, becomes considerably narrower and crosses other paths, heading continually towards the summit that looms in front. On reaching the stones that crown the summit it veers first left and later right, becomes faint in places and some scrambling is needed, though this is made easy because the rock slabs are so large. The summit is marked by a large cairn, shelter and triangulation pillar Ⓑ, from where there is a magnificent panoramic view up and down the north and south coasts of the Lleyn Peninsula, along the western edge of Snowdonia and across to Anglesey.

Now make for the third peak, which

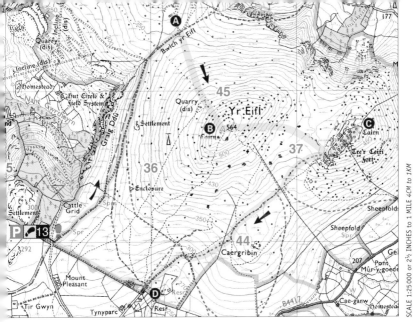

can be clearly seen to the east, 1,591ft (485m) high and crowned by the ramparts of its Iron Age fort. Head towards it, following a narrow but discernible path that heads downhill, bearing slightly to the left all the time. Where the path forks just below the summit of the central peak continue along the left-hand path (even though the right-hand one looks the clearer), at one stage passing below huge boulders on the left before bearing away from them steeply downhill into the valley between the two peaks. From here continue across a flat area of rough grass which is likely to be boggy, but keep in a straight line, making for a path that can be seen ahead snaking up the hillside.

After picking up this path, which soon starts to climb, bear right and then left through a gap in the outer walls of the Iron Age fort of Tre'r Ceiri, which occupies the summit of the hill. Its remains are among the most impressive in Wales – a series of defensive walls within which are a large number of hut circles. Follow a path more steeply now between rocks, go through another gap in the walls and turn left up to the summit cairn **C**, passing the remains of

many of the hut circles on the way.

From here there is another magnificent panoramic view – the village of Llanaelhaearn lies below.

Retrace your steps to where you entered the outer walls of the fort and turn left to follow a downhill path through the valley between the central and eastern peaks. Bear slightly right on joining a broader path and at the next fork take the narrower right-hand path which continues down to a wall. Climb a ladder-stile, just to the right of a gate, and continue along a clear path which as it descends reveals more fine views in front of the coastlines and the rolling hills of Lleyn.

Climb another ladder-stile, continue towards the village of Llithfaen and about 200yds before the nearest house bear right onto a path **D**, which soon crosses a track and heads over open grassland towards another house. Turn right along a track in front of the house and follow it back to the starting point, keeping by a wall on the left all the way. ●

Conwy Mountain and Sychnant Pass

		GPS waypoints	
Start	Conwy town centre	✏	SH 783 775
Distance	6 miles (9.5km)	Ⓐ	SH 773 777
Height gain	1,215 feet (370m)	Ⓑ	SH 758 777
Approximate time	3 hours	Ⓒ	SH 750 770
Parking	Car parks in Conwy (Pay and Display)	Ⓓ	SH 759 762
Route terrain	Mostly rough upland tracks or farmland; some road walking		
Ordnance Survey maps	Landranger 115 (Snowdon/Yr Wyddfa), Explorer OL17 (Snowdon/Yr Wyddfa)		

Perhaps it is not surprising that Conwy Mountain is one of the most popular walking areas along the North Wales coast; its breezy, gorse- and bracken-laden slopes offer a range of delights from ease of access, starting in one of the country's historic towns, to clear paths, easy walking and splendid panoramic views in virtually all directions. There are numerous pathways on Conwy Mountain, allowing visitors to create many variations. This route rises to the top of the mountain before dropping to the Sychnant Pass and returning to Conwy through farmland pastures.

Conwy is an ancient market town, and arguably one of the best medieval walled towns in Europe. Edward I built his castle here between 1283 and 1289 as part of his conquest of Wales, one of a chain of 17 castles encircling Snowdonia. During Edward's time only the English were allowed to live within the walls, or to run a business. The Welsh had to live outside, and could pursue occupations only as farmers or shepherds.

Within the town's walls lie a number of interesting buildings: the 14th-century church occupying the site of the Cistercian abbey of Aberconway, moved by King Edward when he built

his castle; Aberconwy House, a 13th-century merchant's house, and the impressive 16th-century town house, Plas Mawr. The nearby suspension bridge is the handiwork of Thomas Telford, who completed the construction in 1826, replacing the ferry that plied across the Afon Conwy at this point. The adjacent tubular railway bridge is the work of Robert Stephenson, built along the Chester to Holyhead railway line in 1849.

You need to leave Conwy, seemingly by setting off in the wrong direction, walking onto the quayside, there turning left and soon passing the Smallest House in Britain, Quay House, which measures a mere 3.05m x 1.8m, and has been lived in since the 16th century.

Continue along the quayside and out through the town wall, as far as a road junction. Here, bear right onto the North Wales Path, a 60-mile romp from Bangor to Prestatyn. This soon becomes a surfaced path leading along the water's edge. Follow the path to its conclusion at another road junction, and there turn left to walk out to meet the A547 close by a convenient pedestrian crossing. Cross into the road opposite, and go over the bridge spanning the railway line, then press on along a walled track to a surfaced lane and then a road junction.

At the junction, turn right, climbing gently past houses, and when the rising track levels and then forks, branch right to a ladder-stile  giving onto Conwy Mountain. The path now climbs through bracken, flanked by beech and gorse,

SCALE 1:25 000 or 2½ INCHES to 1 MILE 4CM to 1KM

```
0    200   400   600   800 METRES   1
                                     KILOMETRES
                                     MILES
0    200   400   600 YARDS    ½
```

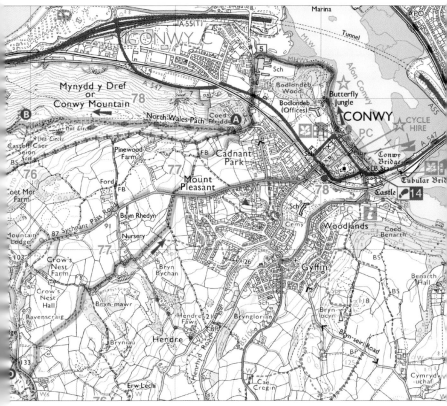

Conwy Castle and estuary from Conwy Mountain

Having crossed the farm access, either go forward onto a broad grassy track traversing a low shoulder, or simply turn left along the access track. Both routes shortly rejoin, and the path then followed to the top of Sychnant Pass (Bwlch Sychnant) **C**.

Cross the road at the pass and climb to a gate in a wall beyond which a gently rising path runs beside a wall, but just as the path passes beneath powerlines, it divides. Branch left onto a narrow path crossing a hill shoulder, and parallel with a wall. Soon the path descends to a wall corner. Over this, go forward to a small group of lakes (Gwern Engen), and then keep on in the same direction to reach another rough track. Turn right to a junction near a group of buildings, and then bear left, to descend steeply to a narrow lane **D**.

Turn right and pass Ty Coch farm, and at Y Bwthyn, the next house, leave the lane by turning left through a gate onto an enclosed path that shortly breaks out into a field. Stride across this towards a vehicle track, cross it, and go through a gate. Now follow an obvious route across fields linked by gates, finally targeting a tree in a fence corner not far from a small wooded hill, and then keep on to reach another lane.

Turn right and follow the lane past Oakwood Park Hall to a T-junction. Turn right, briefly, and then go left at a signpost, and across fields to a gate. Through this bear left along the field margin to reach the Sychnant Pass road. Now all that remains is to turn right and follow the road back to Conwy. ●

and climbs energetically for a while with improving views to the south and east. At a waymark pole, leave the North Wales Path by branching right to intercept a wide, grassy path along the spine of the mountain; turn left along this and following, as closely as possible, the actual crest of the mountain. Always sticking to the high ground, and ignoring deviating paths, you come finally to the top of the mountain **B**.

The top of Conwy Mountain is occupied by Neolithic hut circles and Castell Caer Seion, an Iron Age stone-walled hill fort. The numerous remains and excavations show that this was an extensive site, and you can still pick out the remains of over fifty hut circles and platforms, with a citadel and outposts.

Cross the top of the mountain, but then gradually descend through a scatter of low hills at the western end of the mountain, progressively moving to the landward side of the mountain. The path comes down to meet a broad track at a North Wales Path waymark. Keep forward and make another short ascent before the path drops to a ford and stepping stones not far from Pen-pyra farm.

Loggerheads and Cilcain

		GPS waypoints
Start	Loggerheads Country Park	
Distance	6½ miles (10.5km)	✎ SJ 197 626
Height gain	890 feet (270m)	**A** SJ 189 637
		B SJ 177 649
Approximate time	3 hours	**C** SJ 171 647
Parking	Car park at start	**D** SJ 168 644
Route terrain	Woodland, farmland, some minor roads	**E** SJ 183 634
Ordnance Survey maps	Landranger 117 (Chester and Wrexham), Explorer 265 (Clwydian Range)	

The 80-acre Loggerheads Country Park centres around a beautiful wooded river valley, backed by dramatic cliffs and limestone outcrops; this is great for a short walk and as good a place as any to begin an exploration of the Clwydian Range. You soon realise that this was formerly an important lead mining area, and evidence of this industrial legacy will be encountered in a few places as you wander through the woodland.

✎ The walk begins in the company of the River Alyn (Afon Alun), which has a surprising connection with the German composer, Felix Mendelssohn. He is known to have stayed at nearby Coed Du Hall, at Rhydymwyn, as a guest of John Taylor, a mining engineer and entrepreneur, and the third of his three Fantasies for piano ('The Rivulet': Opus 16, No. 3), composed as gifts for Taylor's daughters Anne, Susan and Honora, evokes the River Alyn, where Mendelssohn and the girls sometimes stopped to rest during walks and horseback rides.

From the car park, head towards the visitor centre, shop and **café**, continuing past them to cross a bridge over the river. Turn left, below the impressive limestone cliffs of Pen y Clogwyn. The path leads on through pleasant woodland, following the true right bank of the river.

At a track junction (signpost), keep to the path for Cilcain and the Devil's Gorge. Keep on to pass an isolated property (cattery and kennels) and go forward on the Leete Path. A broad vehicle track leads on into an ascending surfaced lane, at which point, cross to a woodland path opposite **A**.

When the path divides at a waymark, keep to the lower path, and press on in due course to pass the impressive gash that is the Devil's Gorge. Remain on the continuing Leete Path, now high above the river and at various times at the base of limestone cliffs. Follow the path until eventually it emerges onto a road. Turn left, descending to cross a road bridge spanning the Alyn.

Now, follow the road, ignore branching footpaths, and climb briskly until the road swings sharply to the right, and here leave it on the apex, at a wooden footpath sign (for Pentre and

Cilcain). Walk up to a stile, and beyond, continue along the left edge of a paddock to another stile. Press on, at the edge of a steep slope down to a tributary of the Alyn, to a third stile and a level path beyond.

At a stile, where the path divides again, keep forward for Pentre, still remaining throughout above the slope down to the river. At the next path junction, again at a signpost, keep left for Pentre-Cilcain, now along a narrow path above the river. The path descends to a point close by a narrow footbridge. Ignore the bridge, and instead bear right on an ascending sunken path up to a surfaced lane **Ⓑ**.

Anyone wanting to visit the **White Horse** pub in Cilcain, should turn right here, staying on the lane, then turning left at each junction to pass the pub, and, later, rejoin the main route **Ⓒ**.

Otherwise, turn left, descending past Wayside Cottage. Follow the lane downwards, and then, as it climbs and swings to the left, leave it by branching right onto a much narrower lane, passing Cross Foxes Farm, and leading to a road junction at which the lane from Cilcain is met **Ⓒ**. Here, leave the

lane by going forward and then immediately left through a gate onto a rough farm track. Within a few strides, leave the track by crossing a high stone stile on the right, and then go forward along the left-hand field edge, and maintain the same direction across fields until the route emerges via a stile

Loggerheads Country Park with Moel Famau on the horizon

in the far left corner of a field, onto a broad track, near a track junction **D**.

Turn left onto a broad track, soon cross a shallow ford and go through a bridlegate, and climb up to another gate, there keeping forward alongside a fence. Cross a section of boardwalk and onto a gently rising path below a line of ancient hawthorn. Keep forward past a farm and out along a vehicle track.

On the way, you pass a brick structure on the right. This was a small decoy site, built during the Second World War to protect the valley water works.

Keep following the track until it emerges onto a narrow lane **E**. Here, turn left, descending to a T-junction. Cross the road, and onto an enclosed footpath that leads steeply down via stiles to a footbridge spanning the River Alyn. Over the bridge, tackle an awkward little ascent on the right, across limestone (slippery when wet), and, at the top, turn right to retrace the outward route back to the Loggerheads car park. ●

SCALE 1:25000 or 2½ INCHES to 1 MILE 4CM to 1KM

```
0     200   400   600   800 METRES  1
                                    KILOMETRES
                                    MILES
0     200   400   600 YARDS   ½
```

Moel Famau

		GPS waypoints
Start	Moel Famau woodland car park	✐ SJ 172 611
Distance	5¼ miles (8.25km)	Ⓐ SJ 162 605
Height gain	1,265 feet (385m)	Ⓑ SJ 161 626
Approximate time	3 hours	Ⓒ SJ 168 616
Parking	Car park at start (Honesty box, and Pay and Display)	Ⓓ SJ 163 615
Route terrain	Woodland, open heather moorland	
Ordnance Survey maps	Landranger 116 (Denbigh and Colwyn Bay), Explorer 265 (Clwydian Range)	

Moel Famau is the highest hill in the Clwydian Range, on the border between Denbighshire and Flintshire. The hill, gives its name to the Moel Famau Country Park, and has been central to the Clwydian Range and Dee Valley Area of Outstanding Natural Beauty since 1985, and, for hill baggers, is classed as a Marilyn.

The walk has two distinct parts, beginning and finishing through woodland and plantations, but with a fine stretch of the Offa's Dyke Path between the two, an interlude that offers fine, far-reaching views of the Denbigh moorlands and the distant mountains of Snowdonia.

✐ Start from the car park by walking out to the road, and turning right, up towards Bwlch Penbarras. After about 250yds, leave the road by bearing left onto a wide forest trail, known locally as the Mushroom Path. This is a gentle start, rising gradually at an easy angle to the large car park at the pass Ⓐ; bear right to the road.

Cross the road, keeping left, and start up the broad track that is now the Offa's Dyke Path (signposted for 'Jubilee Tower'). When the track forks, keep left along the lower path, a delightful terraced path flanked by gorse. Views of undulating, rolling hills appear beyond the Clwyd valley and the towns of

Ruthin, with its ancient castle/hotel, and Denbigh. To the south, Foel Fenlli is prominent, and, like Bron-y-felin to the west, was the site of an Iron Age hill fort. The walking is gentle and invigorating, easing steadily upwards in easy stages with numerous benches on which to rest, to a final pull to the Jubilee Tower that crowns the top of Moel Famau Ⓑ.

The tower was built in 1810 to commemorate the Golden Jubilee of George III, and was designed like a three-tiered Egyptian obelisk. However, the tower was never completed because of a lack of funds. In 1862, a storm brought down the incomplete tower, following which the remaining upper part of the structure was demolished for safety reasons leaving just the base, the alcoves of which provide shelter from all but the most persistent winds.

Leaving the summit of Moel Famau can be problematical in poor visibility. A trig pillar stands forlornly nearby and beyond it a gate giving onto heather moorland. Ignore this direction, but look for another gate a little more to the south-east (to the right of the trig pillar), and through this soon engage a steep, shaly path descending quickly to the shelter of the plantation below.

Press on down through the plantation, once more steeply, to reach a waymark post at a path junction **Ⓒ**. *From here, by continuing to descend, you will be led directly back to the car park, should it be necessary to abbreviate the walk.* At the waymark, turn right (blue waymark with white spot), descending on a narrow path to reach a track junction, with trails going in a number of directions. Ignore trails going right and left, and keep forward on a broad track, initially open, that swings slightly to the right. Follow this for about 250yds, and when the track divides **Ⓓ**, bear left (white waymark).

The track curves around through the upper reaches of the plantation, and eventually drops easily towards Bwlch Penbarras. Just before reaching the road, swing acutely left through a gate and onto a descending gravel path that, ignoring branching paths, leads all the way back down to the start. ●

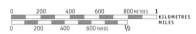

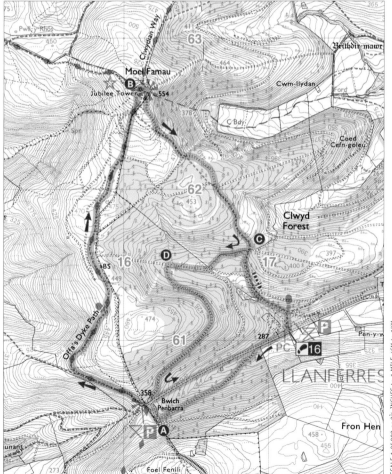

SCALE 1:25000 or 2½ INCHES to 1 MILE 4CM to 1KM

Llyn Dinas and Cwm Bychan

Start	Beddgelert
Distance	6 miles (9.5km)
Height gain	1,340 feet (410m)
Approximate time	3½ hours
Parking	Car park near Royal Goat Hotel (Pay and Display)
Route terrain	Riverside trails, mountain upland, riverside gorge
Ordnance Survey maps	Landranger 115 (Snowdon), Explorer OL17 (Snowdon/Yr Wyddfa)

GPS waypoints

- ✐ SH 588 481
- Ⓐ SH 604 489
- Ⓑ SH 612 492
- Ⓒ SH 604 482
- Ⓓ SH 597 462

There are three distinct sections to this walk. The first, low-level and leading by a delightful trail to the edge of Llyn Dinas; the second section engages a stiff climb into the folds of the crags above, heather-purple in summer, and then down through the delights of Cym Bychan, while the final stretch takes to a rocky gorge and a fisherman's path leading back to Beddgelert.

✐ From the car park near the **Royal Goat Hotel**, walk out to the road and turn left towards the bridge spanning the Afon Colwyn. Just before the bridge, turn right onto a lane parallel with the river (signposted to Gelert's Grave). At the turning for Gelert's Grave, keep forward over Glaslyn Bridge, and on the other side, bear left to pass the left-hand edge of a row of terraced cottages.

Cross a lane at the next bridge, and then continue through a kissing-gate onto the Riverside Walk, to follow a gravel path through an area of rhododendron and gorse, which leads to a ladder-stile giving on to a narrow lane.

Walk along the lane, towards the Victorian Sygun Copper Mine, closed in 1903, but re-opened as a tourist attraction in 1986. On approaching the mine, leave the lane by branching left

through bracken and in front of a cottage to the access lane to the mine. Turn left through a wide wall gap and walk down towards a nearby bridge Ⓐ, but without crossing the bridge bear right along a riparian path that leads agreeably on to pass through a gate and so reach the shore of Llyn Dinas.

Bear immediately right onto a stepped, stony path Ⓑ, rising through a spread of bracken, heather and bilberry. After a steep ascent, the gradient eases as the path enters a vast hummocky hollow. Follow the path, for a while the gradient less demanding, and then climb again to arrive at a three-way signpost at Bwlch y Sygyn Ⓒ, close by the spill from copper mine workings.

Turn left at the signpost for Aberglaslyn, following a path through banks of heather that leads to a ladder-stile spanning a fence. Cross the stile

and now go forward and down into
neatly framed Cwm Bychan.

The walk down Cwm Bychan is
enchanting, a lovely natural garden. It
was here in Cwm Bychan that scenes
from the 1958 film, *The Inn of the Sixth
Happiness*, starring Ingrid Bergman,
were filmed. The film was the true story
of Gladys Aylward (1902-1970), who
became a missionary to China during
the years leading up to World War II.

Lower down you enter woodland, but
as you pass into a woodland clearing, a
bridge supporting a railway line invites
you through. On the other side, you
soon reach a car park at Nantmor **D**, an
alternative starting point should
Beddgelert seem unduly busy.

Just beyond a toilet block, a gate

gives onto a path going left for Pont Aberglaslyn, climbing through bracken above the road. Go as far as the bridge, but do not cross it. Instead, take to an undulating fisherman's path on the right, and along the true left bank of the Afon Glaslyn; proximity to the river often means that conditions underfoot can be slippery.

En route through the gorge, you pass the entrance to an old mine tunnel, best not explored; it is flooded for some considerable distance. A short way further on, a short section has had iron hand holds fixed into a rock, but suddenly you are through the gorge and the onward route to Beddgelert opens up, running parallel with the railway.

Eventually you reach a point where you need to cross the railway. Continue beyond, crossing the nearby footbridge spanning the river, and walk easily onward along a surfaced path to Beddgelert to complete the walk. ●

Llyn Dinas

Penycloddiau and Moel Arthur

Start	Moel Famau Country Park
Distance	7½ miles (12km)
Height gain	1,675 feet (510m)
Approximate time	3½ hours
Parking	Coed Llangwyfan car park: 1 mile east of Llangwyfan village
Route terrain	Heather and mountain moorland
Ordnance Survey maps	Landranger 116 (Denbigh and Colwyn Bay), Explorer 265 (Clwydian Range)

GPS waypoints

🖊 SJ 139 667
Ⓐ SJ 121 689
Ⓑ SJ 130 664
Ⓒ SJ 140 656
Ⓓ SJ 147 657

The first and last parts of the route involve two ascents and descents as you follow Offa's Dyke Path along the ridge of the Clwydian Hills, passing the prehistoric hill forts of Penycloddiau and Moel Arthur. The remainder is along clearly defined and generally flat tracks that contour along the side of the hills, making for easy, attractive and trouble-free walking. There are some pleasant wooded stretches and continuously fine views across the broad Vale of Clwyd.

🖊 Begin by going through a gate; at the fork in front take the right-hand track and at the next fork a few strides ahead, take the right-hand, uphill path, following Offa's Dyke Path waymarks. The path runs parallel to the track and heads uphill, steeply at times, along the right edge of conifers to a stile.

Turn right over the stile, here crossing the outer earth-works of Penycloddiau, an Iron Age hill fort, and continue uphill across the middle of the fort. After passing a cairn, you reach the outer defences again and at this point the views from this ridge top track, to the right and left and ahead along the undulating Clwydian range, are of rolling hills and far, purpled heather moorlands. Bear right for a few yards and then turn left to continue across moorland, descending to a stile. Climb it, cross a low rise and then continue gradually downhill on the wide path, following Offa's Dyke Path waymarks to another stile Ⓐ just beyond a stand of pine trees.

Do not climb this stile, but turn left on to a broad track by a wire fence on the right. Keep along this winding track for the next 2½ miles, passing through several gates, and at one stage by the edge of attractive woodland, and with agreeable views across the Vale of Clwyd all the time. Finally the track bears left and keeps below conifers to reach a lane Ⓑ.

Bear left, follow the lane around a right-hand bend and where it bends to the left, turn right at a public bridleway sign, along a track. This is another

1¾ miles, you go through a metal gate on to a lane **G**, turn left and follow the lane as far as Moel Arthur car park **D**.

Near the far end of the car park use the gap in the wall on the left, indicated by a fingerpost 'Offa's Dyke Path & Llangwyfan Wood,' and join a steepening path that curls through bracken and heather around the eastern flank of Moel Arthur. As the path levels, a short diversion can be made (left) to explore this fine Iron Age hill fort.

On the shoulder of Moel Arthur

curving, partially wooded track that you follow through several more gates and from which there are again superb views over the Vale to be enjoyed. After

To reach the finish line, simply remain on the well-used Offa's Dyke Path, descending steadily via three stiles to gain a lane just a few paces downhill from the car park. ●

A pleasant track in the Clwydian Hills

Mynydd Mawr

		GPS waypoints
Start	Rhyd Ddu	🥾 SH 571 526
Distance	6¼ miles (10km)	Ⓐ SH 569 529
Height gain	1,805 feet (550m)	Ⓑ SH 563 541
Approximate time	4 hours	Ⓒ SH 548 544
Parking	Car park at start, adjacent to the Rhyd Ddu station	
Route terrain	Mountain upland; some steep slopes	
Ordnance Survey maps	Landranger 115 (Snowdon/Yr Wyddfa), Explorer OL17 (Snowdon/Yr Wyddfa)	

Wearing rose-coloured spectacles and with a modicum of imagination, Mynydd Mawr, viewed from Anglesey, takes on the profile of a recumbent elephant. Without the spectacles, it is simply a big mountain. This rather neglected outlier, barring northward approaches into the Nantlle valley, does not lend itself to circular walks, but this simple romp up and down by the same route is as good as anything, and provides a grandstand view of Anglesey and the north-western coastline of Wales.

🥾 Exit the northern edge of the car park and, opposite a railway crossing, take a broad track to the left between cottages to walk out to the village road. Turn right, and go as far as the road for Nantlle, there turning left. Just after a speed de-restriction sign, leave the road by branching right onto a broad trail Ⓐ into the northern arm of the Beddgelert Forest.

Follow the pleasant trail through the plantation, until you arrive at an area where the forest has been cleared. Down below, Llyn Cwellyn eases into view against a backdrop of the bosomy Moel Eilio and its neighbours.

A path climbs from Planwydd Farm, rising to meet the forest trail Ⓑ. Here the on-going path, as it now is, divides. Climb left, taking the higher of two paths, up through the remaining plantation to arrive at a ladder-stile

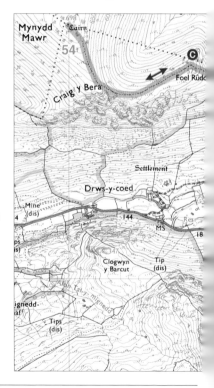

spanning a fence at the top boundary of the plantation.

Ahead now lies the Nantlle valley, the Nantlle Ridge and the steep slopes of Mynydd Mawr along which the crags of Craig y Bera are starting to take form. In the foreground Clogwynygarreg, a volcanic plug or *roche moutonnée*, is quite dramatic, rising above the obviously drained area that once housed Llyn Bwlch y Moch. To the south, looking towards distant Moel Hebog, lies the fabled Llyn y Dywarchen.

Llyn y Dywarchen was remarked upon by Gerald of Wales in his *Journey through Wales* as possessing a floating island. Over time, this marvel became legend, although, with the righteous faith of a cleric, Gerald offered a rational explanation: 'It is possible that a section of the bank was broken off in times long past and that, bound together in a natural way by the roots of the willows and other shrubs which grow there, it has since become larger by alluvial deposits. It is continually driven from one bank to another by the violent winds.'

Subsequent travellers, up to 600 years later, have remarked on the island, including the famous astronomer Halley, who swam out to it in 1698 to satisfy himself that it existed.

Over the ladder-stile, turn right beside the fence and walk to another a short distance away. Beyond this, a narrow path crosses a low shoulder and then sets about tackling the long haul up onto Mynydd Mawr. The path tackles huge and steep grassy slopes, and rises to another stile close by the top edge of the plantation. From here a steep ascent over grass and minor rock outcrops leads to the top of Foel Rudd **C**, a minor summit but one that suddenly

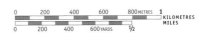

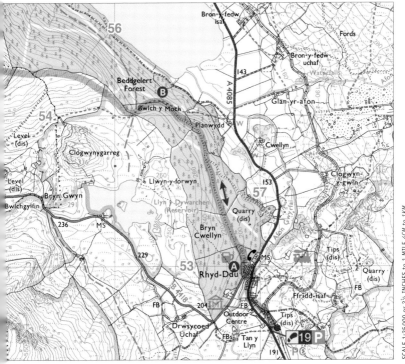

The Snowdon massif viewed from near the summit of Mynydd Mawr

brings the vast hollow of Cwm Planwydd into view; it is quite a stunning moment, with Mynydd Mawr rising smoothly on the other side.

All the steepness now is over, and the final stretch is outstanding, a delicious amble along a clear path that whizzes above the topmost rocks of Craig y Bera, steadily making its way to the top of the mountain, reached over close-clipped turf interspersed with small scatters of stone, although the highest ground is covered by a rash of stones and boulders, and marked by three shelters and a large cairn on the highest point.

As you approach the summit, especially in poor visibility, make a mental note of the line of your approach, as the return path is not visible from the top.

Throughout the walk the undulations of the Nantlle Ridge have remained in view to the south, and these inviting hills now lie across the skyline, an inviting fresco. Northwards the view spans Anglesey, while to the north-west you gaze over the Moel Eilio group to Elidir Fawr and the higher Carneddau beyond.

Once satisfied with your visit to Mynydd Mawr, simply retrace your steps and hope that your knees can take the strain. ●

Tal y Fan

		GPS waypoints
Start	Rowen	📍 SH 760 719
Distance	7¼ miles (11.7km)	**Ⓐ** SH 756 719
Height gain	1,995 feet (610m)	**Ⓑ** SH 731 714
Approximate time	4 hours	**Ⓒ** SH 727 723
Parking	Roadside parking at lower end of Rowen village; please park considerately	**Ⓓ** SH 729 726
		Ⓔ SH 751 737
Route terrain	Minor road walking; mountain and farm upland	**Ⓕ** SH 757 727
Ordnance Survey maps	Landranger 115 (Snowdon/Yr Wyddfa), Explorer OL17 (Snowdon/Yr Wyddfa)	

Tal y Fan is the most north-easterly of the Carneddau peaks, overlooking Conwy and the coast. At just 2,000ft (610m) it is also the lowest mountain in Snowdonia, and the ideal introduction for those who want to climb a mountain without excessive effort. This is also a walk of great historic interest, initially following the line of a Roman road, passing prehistoric monuments and visiting a tiny medieval church in a lovely and remote setting. Despite its relative ease, this is a walk to be **attempted only in good weather**: in misty conditions route-finding could be difficult, especially across the summit of Tal y Fan.

The village of Rowen, on the western side of the Conwy valley, makes an attractive starting point for the walk.

📍 Begin by walking through the village, passing the **Gwesty Ty Gwyn** pub, and turn right at the first road junction **Ⓐ**. Follow a lane uphill by houses, becoming narrower and steeper. At a junction, keep ahead up the 'Dead End'; the lane drops momentarily before climbing increasingly steeply to pass the Rhiw youth hostel. Continue uphill along what is a pleasant, enclosed track, following the line of a Roman road that ran between the forts of Canovium (Caerhun) in the Conwy valley and Segontium (Caernarfon) via the Bwlch y Ddeufaen (a mountain pass). Go

through a metal gate and continue, now less steeply, passing a burial chamber (Maen-y-Bard/Bard's Stone) on the right, then a standing stone a little farther on (on the other side of the wall on the left) and, after passing through two metal gates in quick succession, another standing stone a little farther ahead on the right. It is probably from these that the pass gets its name, as Bwlch y Ddeufaen means 'the Pass of Two Stones'. Continue through another metal gate, shortly joining a tarmac lane which comes in from the left.

About 100yds after joining this lane turn right over a ladder-stile **Ⓑ** and head straight up the hill in front along a path through gorse bushes and to a

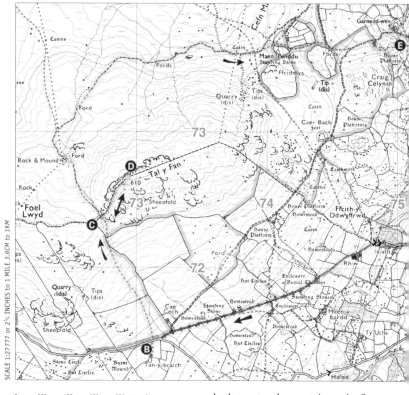

SCALE 1:27777 or 2¼ INCHES to 1 MILE 3.6CM to 1KM

```
0    200    400    600    800 METRES   1
                                        KILOMETRES
                                        MILES
0    200    400    600 YARDS   ½
```

ladder-stile ahead. Climb it and continue steadily uphill, drawing close to and keeping parallel to a wall on the right. Turn right over a ladder-stile in that wall, immediately turn left and head uphill before bearing away from the wall and continuing between rocks and heather to reach one more ladder-stile **C**.

Climb it and turn right for a ½-mile detour from the main route to the summit of Tal y Fan, following a path that climbs between boulders and heather, keeping parallel to a wall on the right, the path becoming increasingly steep and rocky towards the summit. The summit cairn is just on the other side of the wall and can be reached by a stile **D**. The magnificent all-round view from here has the best of

both coast and mountains – the Conwy valley, Conwy town and castle, Conwy Mountain, Llandudno and the Great Orme, the Clwydian Hills, the North Wales coast, Anglesey and the Carneddau range.

Return to the ladder-stile at **C** and turn right along a path that initially skirts the base of rocks on the right and then continues ahead across heather. From now on the path is not very clear and route-finding can be confusing because of the number of sheep tracks, but the path is recognisable most of the time and keeps in a slightly north-westerly direction, just above a shallow, boggy valley on the left and heading directly towards the distant quarry above Penmaenmawr. You'll pass between two low, rocky hillocks and drop slightly left to a boggy area. Pick a way through, cross the brook and look for a well-defined path that still draws

you towards the quarry, before gradually bending right, putting Tal y Fan off to your right. Pass by a low hillock crowned with spiky rocks and remain on the obvious path to re-cross the brook, now continue in the same direction towards Conwy Mountain.

Keep to the right of a circular enclosure, heading gently downhill and curving slightly to the right to continue, now in an easterly direction. The path is boggy in places and crosses several small streams tumbling down from Tal y fan. Pass to the right of another burial chamber (Maen-Penddu) and continue 150yds to a major junction of grassy paths. Bear half-right, aiming to use the left one of the three grassy paths that disappears over a low pass. Keep left on a grassy path coming in from the right, to find a large standing stone to your right beside the path near to ruined buildings. In front is a superb view over the Conwy valley to the horizon of the Clwydian Range. Turn right on a narrow path heading for a gate in a wall. Do not go through this but, rather, turn left alongside the wall and trace this through marshy country. As this wall bends away to the right, keep ahead and follow another wall, again putting this on your right.

The path develops into a rough field road, shortly passing through a meeting of walls at a ford. Keep straight ahead from here across reedy pasture to join a wider grassy track coming in from the right. Bear left to find and use two gates immediately beside a set of sheep-pens. Beyond these, the sunken track drops gently to a fork, keep ahead to walk towards the St Celyn's church at Llangelynin. Notice a ladder-stile on your left before reaching the church – this is your mark to return to. It is well worth visiting the remote little church, hardly changed since it was built in the 12th century.

Return to the ladder-stile **E** (now on your right). Do not climb it but, rather, turn left to use a ladder-stile beside a gate. You're now in a reedy, boggy pasture with a wall to your right. Curve gradually away from this and pass well left of a ruined barn to find two ladder-stiles in a cross wall. Climb the left-hand one and walk ahead, a ruinous wall on your right, eventually passing above a ruined building. Just a few steps beyond this, turn right through a gap in a wall and head half-right and downhill into the funnel-like, steep pasture dotted with trees. You need to turn right perhaps 30yds before the old fence at the woodland edge and look carefully for a ladder-stile (it is difficult to spot but persevere) sited between two parallel streams. Climb this and walk ahead to join a rough old track, turning down along it.

Pass above a barn and swing sharp left, then almost immediately turn right at a post (50 paces before the farmyard gate), walking on damp ground beneath alders to a field gate. Turn left in front of this and use the nearby ladder-stile to access a farm road. Walk ahead down this, passing by a cottage to reach a lane **F**. Bear right along the lane for ½ mile, heading up to a T-junction to rejoin the outward route. Turn left and retrace your steps to Rowen. ●

Monumental cross near Llyn Geirionydd

Aberdaron and Land's End

Start	Aberdaron	GPS waypoints
Distance	7½ miles (12km). Shorter version 6½ miles (10.5km)	✐ SH 172 264
		Ⓐ SH 166 263
		Ⓑ SH 163 255
Height gain	1,280 feet (390m)	Ⓒ SH 156 243
Approximate time	4½ hours	Ⓓ SH 144 256
Parking	Car park at start	Ⓔ SH 139 258
Route terrain	Coastal margins, sometimes rocky; farmland; narrow lanes	Ⓕ SH 151 258
Ordnance Survey maps	Landranger 123 (Lleyn Peninsula), Explorer 253 (Lleyn Peninsula West)	

This splendid coastal walk from Aberdaron to the tip of the Lleyn Peninsula follows in the footsteps of medieval pilgrims on their way to Bardsey Island. The views are superb – along the coasts of Lleyn, across to Bardsey Island, and inland. The shorter version omits Mynydd Mawr. This walk is not recommended in strong winds, and although it is not strenuous there are a few places where the coastal path is narrow and slippery and care is needed.

The remote village of Aberdaron is a delightful place. A collection of cottages, pubs, cafés and shops cluster above the beach and up the hill leading into the village, presided over by a small medieval church with a fine Norman doorway. For the medieval pilgrims to Bardsey Island, Aberdaron was the last stopping place, and the 14th-century **Y-Gegin Fawr** ('the Old Kitchen') which gave them food and shelter appropriately retains a similar function as a café for today's visitors.

✐ If the tide is out, a short walk along the beach will bring you to Port Simdde Ⓐ, reached from the car park by crossing the hump-back bridge over the River Daron, keeping ahead and turning right along the shore. Alternatively, begin by turning left out of the car park and head up the road signposted Porth Oer/Whistling Sand. Climb the hill to reach a metal kissing-gate on the left at a National Trust sign. Go through this to a wooden gate and follow the field boundary, keeping the fence on your left, to a wooden kissing-gate. Wooden steps then take you down to Porth Simdde Ⓐ, cross the wooden bridge and bear right at the old kissing-gate along the waymarked Wales Coast Path. All the way along this well waymarked path, that threads its way between gorse, there are splendid views to the left across the bay.

After passing through two wooden kissing-gates drop down to Porth Meudwy Ⓑ and continue up steps on the other side, to regain the cliff top. This section of the path is clear and easy to follow but as it is also narrow and rather worn and crumbly in places care is needed. Continue above a succession of steep-sided coves, negotiating some rocks at one point, climb a stile, and after passing the last of the series of coves (Hen Borth) take the right-hand higher path at a fork, keeping parallel to a wall on the left a little way ahead. (Do not take the slightly lower path nearer the cliff edge.) The distinct path rises gradually across the windy, bracken and heather-strewn headland of Pen y Cil towards the exposed rocks near the cliff edge.

On reaching the top of the cliffs there is a sheer drop below and the first view of Bardsey Island across the treacherous waters of Bardsey Sound. Turn right to climb through the rocks to the top of the headland, making towards the cairn at the summit of Pen y Cil **C**, a superb viewpoint.

Continue past the cairn and the National Trust plaque to pick up a clear, broad path, following it to a metal kissing-gate. Through the gate, turn left to a metal gate and footpath sign, go through the gate and continue along the right-hand edge of a field, by a bank and wire fence on the right, in the direction of the prominent hill of Mynydd Mawr ('Big Mountain'). Go through a metal kissing-gate to enter the National Trust property of Bychestyn. Continue by a wall and wire fence on the right, passing through a wooden gate and keep ahead along a

Aberdaron from the coast path

walled track to reach a T-junction.

Turn right along the narrow lane; at a bend in 250yds turn left on a rough farm lane along the finger-posted Lleyn Peninsula Path. Use the metal gate and then the ladder-stile a short way beyond. From here head half-right to another ladder-stile beside a gate. Climb this and turn three-quarters left to use a gateway to the left of an iron barn. This sets you on a fieldside farm access road, simply remain on this, passing straight over a cross-track near another barn, to gain a lane beyond a cattle-grid **D**.

At this point those wishing to do the shorter version omitting Mynydd Mawr should turn right, picking up the full route again in just a few paces where a farm road comes in from the left.

To do the full route turn left along the lane, passing by a cottage and then over a cattle-grid. Remain on the lane as it bends right. In about 70 paces is a low wooden post on the left; here fork off the lane along a wide grassy path that bends gradually right. Join a line of fence to your right; where this ends turn left for 30 paces and then fork right at a low waymarked post along a narrow path rising across the heathery, rocky hillside. This path soon braids, simply keep slightly right and always uphill to reach a concrete platform, the site of a wartime radar station. Climb the wide concrete steps here to rise to the old coastguard lookout station on Mynydd Mawr **E**. An interpretive plaque details its history. More immediate are the potentially immense views, along the Lleyn, across to the heart of Snowdonia and down the sweep of Cardigan Bay to distant Pembrokeshire – on very clear days the Wicklow Mountains in Ireland can be seen. Close to hand are the scant remains of prehistoric stone circles.

Continue along a concrete road which heads downhill, first bending

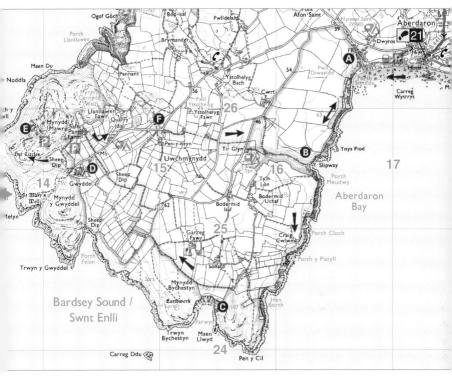

sharply to the right, then bending equally sharply to the left, and where it bends to the right again keep ahead along a faint but discernible path which heads down to a farm. Look out for a small metal kissing-gate down to your right; go through it and continue between the farm buildings and along the tarmac drive ahead to come out on to a lane just a few yards to the left of the earlier route **D**.

Turn left along the lane (*those on the shorter version of the walk will have turned right along it*) for nearly ½ mile. Just past a public footpath sign and where the lane bends to the left **F** bear right along a track in front of Penbryn Bach Restaurant. At the farm use the two gates immediately beside (right of) the house and keep ahead to a kissing-gate in the field corner. Go straight ahead across the pasture to climb a ladder-stile, and continue to another small metal gate. Go through that, descend steps and turn right along a track which leads to a lane. Turn right along the lane for a few yards to a footpath sign; here turn left up some steps to walk along a raised bank, descending steps again at the far end and through a metal gate and a metal kissing-gate onto another lane.

Turn right to Tir Glyn Farm. Turn left down the driveway and trace this through to the campsite toilet block. Slip left immediately past this into a grassy, then earth path that drops (there are some wooden steps) to a metal kissing-gate. Cross the flat bridge beyond this and walk up to a rough lane. Turn right to reach the boat haven at Porth Meudwy **B**. Climb the steps beyond the building on your left to retrace the Wales Coast Path back to Aberdaron.

Melynllyn and Dulyn Reservoirs

		GPS waypoints
Start	Cwm Eigiau	
Distance	5½ miles (9km)	✐ SH 732 663
Height gain	1,175 feet (360m)	Ⓐ SH 720 669
		Ⓑ SH 702 658
Approximate time	4½ hours	Ⓒ SH 702 663
Parking	Car park at start	Ⓓ SH 710 670
Route terrain	Rough upland tracks; steep rocky descent; boggy moorland	Ⓔ SH 716 673
		Ⓕ SH 717 675
Ordnance Survey maps	Landranger 115 (Snowdon/Yr Wyddfa), Explorer OL17 (Snowdon/Yr Wyddfa)	

The two reservoirs secreted into the eastern slopes of the Carneddau are very much out of sight, out of mind; few walkers venture this way. Yet, as this walk reveals, linking the two reservoirs is much more than a walk into the industrial past of North Wales. The walking is generally straightforward throughout, but this is a bleak place in poor weather conditions.

The walk begins high in Cwm Eigiau, accessed by a tortuous road that leaves the B5106 at Tal-y-bont just south of the Bedol pub (not the turning to Llanbedr-y-cennin), and climbs narrowly into the mountain cwm above. Take great care driving up and down this road. Once the farms have been left behind, the road runs arrow-straight to a parking area below the nearby ridge of Cefn-Tal-llyn-Eigiau. The eponymous Llyn Eigiau can be seen to the south-west, tucked into the upper reaches of the valley, backed by the shapely Pen yr Helgi Du and Pen Llithrig y Wrach.

✐ From the parking area, cross a nearby ladder-stile, and walk along a rough, stony track to another gate and stile. Beyond, the track divides. Keep left, ascending, and pass between two huge boulders to follow a rising track

that works its way around the north-eastern end of Cefn-Tal-llyn-Eigiau, en route passing a cluster of sheepfolds.

Press on beyond another gate and stile Ⓐ, after which a steadily rising ascent leads deeper into the cwm, before finally dropping to the ruins and an old iron wheel that mark the site of Hone Quarry, the remains of which can be seen on the hillside above. Follow the track across moorland slopes to reach the reservoir dam Ⓑ.

Melynllyn had a small dam, built in 1887, to provide water power for Hone quarry, but it seems that this was deliberately breached in 1970. The water flows down Afon Melynllyn, which soon joins the Afon Dulyn as it flows down Pant-y-Griafolen.

Onward, cross the outflow stream and pick up an initially indistinct path heading down towards Dulyn Reservoir.

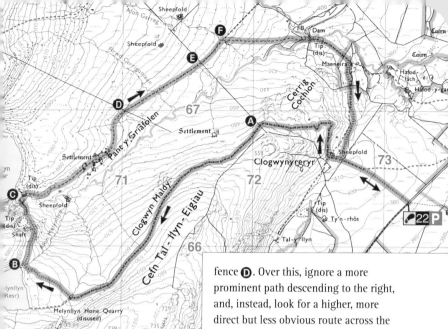

Follow this steadily, to a steep descent on rough-hewn steps that take the route down to the dam remains at Dulyn **C**.

The dam here was built in 1881, but has seen many alterations. The possibility exists here of having to retreat, since the dam overflow needs to be crossed either at its source, or slightly lower down. This is likely to be a problem only after a prolonged period of heavy rainfall. Retreat is the better part of valour, but it is very rare for it not to be possible to cross to a path on the other side that leads to the nearby bothy (Mountain Bothies Association).

Behind the bothy, locate a narrow path heading north-east to pass above the site of an old settlement, today marked by a stand of Scots pine. Thereafter, some boggy moorland awaits. There are a number of variable possibilities impressed into the wet moor, but the line is marked by low concrete posts that mark the course of an underground electricity cable. Press on to a metal ladder-stile spanning a fence **D**. Over this, ignore a more prominent path descending to the right, and, instead, look for a higher, more direct but less obvious route across the moor. Cross another fence/stile **E**, and then keep on along a clearer path for about 250yds to a distinct stream gully, flanked with gorse. This is the Afon Garreg-wen **F**, which can usually be boulder-hopped, although there is a footbridge on the line of the right-of-way.

Once across the bridge, go forward towards another concrete post, but then look for a descending path, diagonally to the right. The path is wet in places and discontinuous but it leads down to an initially concealed building, hidden beside the Afon Ddu. This is the Dulyn Weir Power Station. The station has been operational since 1998, producing 500 kilowatts of green power, and by adopting an innovative engineering solution that enabled electricity to be generated by utilising existing hydroelectric infrastructure, was built primarily to transfer water to Cowlyd reservoir.

Go through a nearby gate, which gives onto a broad track, and now follow this as it skirts the edge of Cerrig Cochion and works a way back to join the outward route near the two large boulders. Retrace your outward steps from here. ●

Llyn Geirionydd
and Llyn Crafnant

		GPS waypoints
Start	Crafnant	
Distance	8½ miles (13.5km)	✏ SH 756 618
Height gain	1,880 feet (575m)	**A** SH 762 624
		B SH 764 615
Approximate time	4½ hours	**C** SH 755 601
Parking	Large car park (Pay and Display;	**D** SH 750 584
	toilets) north-east of the outflow	**E** SH 738 579
	from Llyn Crafnant	**F** SH 732 581
		G SH 738 596
Route terrain	Woodland, riverside paths and	**H** SH 739 603
	tracks; rough mountain tracks	
Ordnance Survey maps	Landranger 115 (Snowdon/Yr Wyddfa),	
	Explorer OL17 (Snowdon/Yr Wyddfa)	

*The parallel valleys that contain Llyn Geirionydd and Llyn
Crafnant are hugely popular at any time of year. This circular
walk, while starting near Llyn Crafnant, soon skips into the
adjacent valley in search of a way through woodlands to join an
ancient track from Capel Curig. This is delightful walking,
threading woodlands, low hills, lakes and streams, and with a
heady tang of wildness that reminds you that rugged mountains
are never far away.*

✏ On leaving the car park, go left
along the road in the direction of
Trefriw, soon walking beside Afon
Crafnant. Walk only as far as a footpath
sign on the right **A**, just before
reaching a cottage (Hendre Isaf). Here,
descend right onto a track that leads to
a bridge spanning the river. On reaching
the bridge, turn left to a narrow
pedestrian bridge nearby, and over this
go forward beside a fence following a
path through bracken to reach a mining
area with ruined buildings and spoil.
This is the Klondyke Mill, and the way
onward is not abundantly clear.

The mill was powered by the river
from Llyn Geirionydd, and apart from
processing its own metals (which

amounted to little) also received lead
and zinc ore from the Pandora mine on
the shores of Geirionydd.

Climb onto the spoil heaps and
locate, on the far right-hand side, a
narrow path into woodland. The path
climbs steadily around the north-
eastern end of Mynydd Deulin, the
Mountain of the Two Lakes, joining one
of the Trefriw Trails. Cross a nearby
ladder-stile, beyond which the path
continues to climb to become a broad,
grassy path across a low shoulder with
Llyn Geirionydd coming gradually into
view. Keep forward on an obvious path,
passing a large monument **B**.

Go past the monument and down
towards the water's edge, where you

find a path running between a wall and the lake.

The lakeside path passes the base of

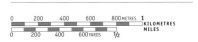

an old mine, after which you climb into light woodland, before returning to the water's edge. At the far end of the lake, pass Ty Newydd, and then cross a stile giving onto a broad track. Here, bear right, following a wide trail as it rises into woodland. The main stands of pine are set back from the trail and fronted by broad-leaved trees, so the walking is very agreeable, and doesn't have any sense of being hemmed in.

When you reach a junction **C**, where the track divides, go left over a step-stile beside a gate, continuing to follow a wide track, but one that now escapes the trees. At another stile you return to a wooded area through which you descend to pass lily-littered Llyn Bychan, a splendid little lake.

Where the track divides at the first turning on the right **D** after Llyn Bychan, swing right into a section of woodland that is now much more enclosed. The track climbs steadily, and then suddenly as you round a bend, Moel Siabod springs into view, framed by trees.

Finally, you leave the woodland at a ladder-stile **E** giving onto a path between a wall and fence, with fine views especially of Moel Siabod, the Snowdon Horseshoe, the Glyderau and the Carneddau. The path is an old sunken track flanked by tumbledown walls that guide you to a step-stile in a fence giving into a brief bout of mainly willow woodland before you emerge onto Access Land, across which the path takes a waymarked route, with the long ridge Crimpiau on your right.

When you intercept a broad track, continue across it, still following a waymarked route along which wooden footbridges span drainage channels. Eventually, the path arrives at a bridge **F**. Do not cross the bridge, but turn immediately right to begin the return to Llyn Crafnant.

Now the path ambles happily through a rocky landscape, working its way up to a high point where the track divides **G**. Branch left, and then go ahead, to pass through an obvious gap to begin the descent to Crafnant. The path slips down through a rugged gorge flanked by rock outcrops, bracken and heather. When this opens up, Creigiau Gleision appears ahead, along with a stunning view of Llyn Crafnant, arguably one of the most satisfying views in Snowdonia.

The path descends steeply for a while to a ladder-stile close by Blaen-y-nant. Take the grassy path leading to the cottage, walk past it and then turn right down a rough access track. After about 100yds, as you reach a large ash tree on the left **H**, just where the track swings to the right, leave it for a grassy path descending through bracken to another cottage, Tan y Manod. Go left on a broad track in front of the cottage, pass another cottage and continue as far as a gate at Hendre, just after which you cross a stream by a footbridge, and climb up into woodland.

Walk up through the woodland for a short distance until, just after a ladder-stile, you intercept a broad track at a waymark. Here, turn right, shortly descending through waterside woodland as it eases past Llyn Crafnant. The track finally emerges at the northern end of the lake onto the valley road. Turn left down this to return to the Crafnant car park.

Crafnant takes its name from 'craf', an old Welsh word for garlic, and 'nant', a stream or valley, an association that is headily evident when the garlic is in bloom. The lake is a reservoir, and dammed at its northern end in 1874, but the dam is barely visible as the out-flow plunges down steeply from it. ●

Llyn Brenig

		GPS waypoints
Start	Llyn Brenig visitor centre	✏ SH 967 546
Distance	9 miles (14.5km)	Ⓐ SH 966 543
Height gain	950 feet (290m)	Ⓑ SH 978 540
Approximate time	4½ hours	Ⓒ SH 983 574
Parking	Car park at start	Ⓓ SH 985 579
Route terrain	Farmland; forest; lakeside paths; some road walking	Ⓔ SH 971 581
		Ⓕ SH 961 571
Ordnance Survey maps	Landranger 116 (Denbigh and Colwyn Bay), Explorer 264 (Vale of Clwyd)	

Llyn Brenig is situated amid the forests and rolling moorlands of Mynydd Hiraethog. This clear and well-waymarked circuit of the reservoir, which mainly uses a mixture of lakeside paths and tracks and forest roads, goes across meadows, over heathery moorland and through the conifer woods of Clocaenog Forest. Although a lengthy walk, the terrain is generally flat and easy, with the likelihood of a few muddy stretches, and there is a succession of fine views across the lake.

✏ Stand facing the lake in front of the visitor centre and turn right, shortly using a hand-gate just above the jetty. This gate is marked with a Clwydian Way disc and also a cream 'walker' disc – these will become familiar as the walk progresses. Walk through to the western end of the stone-clad dam Ⓐ and join the rough road across it.

At the far end Ⓑ turn left, shortly going through a gate. Walk on to a gate and cattle-grid at the edge of the trees, remaining on the rough road through the woods and beyond around a series of inlets. Hairpin sharp left on the main track (there's an isolated old cottage off to the right) and continue above the reservoir. About 150yds before reaching a gate, notice the low, circular stone structure on your left. This is a ring cairn dating from about 4,000 years ago, and used, it is thought, for

funerary rituals. Nearby is a distinct mound – this is Boncyn Arian burial barrow dating from much the same time. Use the stile Ⓒ beside the gate and go ahead beside the car park to join a gently rising tarred lane. You're now at the edge of the Gors-Maen-Llwyd Nature Reserve – there's a bird hide along a path off to your left.

At the top of an incline Ⓓ, look on the left behind a rough lay-by for a waymarked post, here picking up a well-walked path across the moorland. This soon curves around the edge of a wooded area and comes to roughly parallel the main road. There are regular Clwydian Way (CW) posts, although the path is hard to lose.

You'll reach a small, isolated stand of tall ash and short oak trees. Pass immediately left of these and follow the path to a CW post 100yds beyond. From

A corner of Llyn Brenig

here, look ahead to espy a line of blue posts; you should take the very narrow path up past these, leaving the main path to curve away left. There are occasional low wooden steps on this path; eventually you'll reach a larger wooden post with a cream 'walker' disc on. Turn right here and walk the heathery path to reach another such post virtually at the roadside fence **Ⓔ**.

Turn left along the wider, stony path that develops into a track, swinging away from the road and then coming close-by again. There are CW and 'walker' discs confirming the way.

Way off to your right, and well beyond the serried ranks of trees forming Alwen Forest, you should be able to pick out the gaunt, hilltop ruins of Gwylfa Hiraethog. This, 'The Wooden Palace', was built in 1908 as a shooting

lodge by the wealthy Lord Davenport, and was claimed (somewhat disingenuously) to be the highest inhabited building in Britain at that time.

Near a cattle-grid, the path angles away from the road one final time, shortly reaching a hand-gate giving access to this part of Clocaenog Forest. Keep ahead along the forestry road, which shortly becomes tarred. Cross the solid stone bridge over the Afon Brenig and rise to a crossroads **Ⓕ**.

Turn left here with the tarred road, remaining on this as it weaves alongside inlets and along promontories to a junction and a 'No Entry' road sign. Keep ahead here, passing the sailing club to return to the visitor centre car park. ●

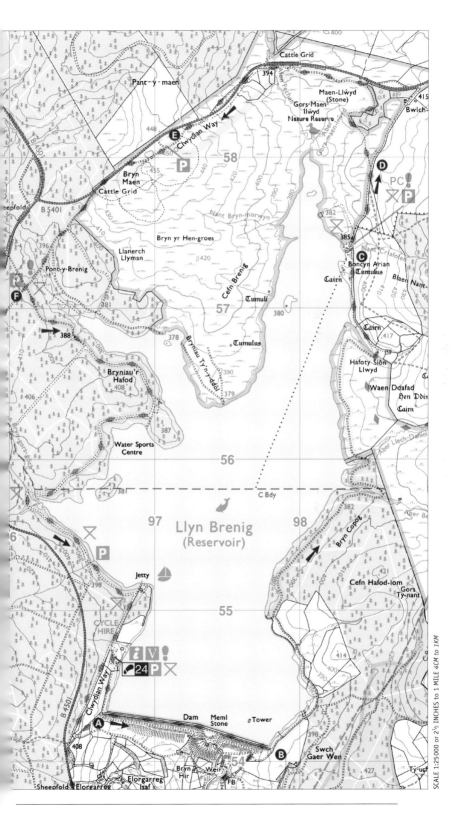

SCALE 1:25000 or 2½ INCHES to 1 MILE 4CM to 1KM

Llantysilio Mountain

Start	Ponderosa Café	GPS waypoints
Distance	7½ miles (12km)	🅐 SJ 192 481
Height gain	1,855 feet (565m)	Ⓐ SJ 180 472
Approximate time	4½ hours	Ⓑ SJ 171 465
Parking	Roadside parking area, opposite the café	Ⓒ SJ 149 451
		Ⓓ SJ 149 460
Route terrain	Heather moorland; farmland; road walking	Ⓔ SJ 151 463
		Ⓕ SJ 168 475
		Ⓖ SJ 171 476
Ordnance Survey maps	Landranger 116 (Denbigh and Colwyn Bay), Explorer 256 (Wrexham & Llangollen)	Ⓗ SJ 174 478

There is little scope for losing one's way on this high-level traverse of Llantysilio Mountain: the track is a wide, gravel blaze through heather moorland, clear enough to follow on a moonlit night. But while the route enjoys clarity and far-reaching views, there is a surprisingly extended series of ups and downs that will call for numerous view-appreciating halts.

🅐 From the roadside car park opposite the **Ponderosa Café** a number of wide, grassy paths rise through the heather, climbing around and above a large quarry; that which heads towards the quarry and then passes to the left

around it is the most direct route to the top of Moel y Faen.

Take the on-going track as it descends, steeply in places, to a broad bwlch (pass)  **A** and then climbs steadily to the highest point on the route, Moel y Gamelin, a neat summit crowned by a large cairn of rocks.

Another steep descent leads to a cross-mountain route **B** used by the Clwydian Way, from where you ascend once more, first to Moel y Gaer, and then up to the trig pillar on Moel Morfydd.

The view is splendid, reaching as far as Winter Hill in Lancashire, and across to the heart of Snowdonia, with Tryfan easily discernible, along with the Glyders, the Carneddau and the Snowdon massif. To the south the tops of the Berwyn Hills poke above intervening heights, while all around heather cloaks the entire hillside, a stunning sight in August and September.

There is evidence for human activity on these hills dating back to at least the Bronze Age, with a large burial cairn on the summit of Moel y Gamelin. Later, during the Iron Age, Moel y Gaer was chosen as the site for a small hill fort. In more recent times these rounded, heathery hills were transformed by extensive slate quarrying, mostly around the Horseshoe Pass, although with smaller quarries dotted around the hillsides. Many quarrymen lived in Rhewl and Llantysilio, walking the hillside tracks to the quarries each day.

Follow the track down from Moel Morfydd, to intercept a lane **C**. Turn right, with fine views on your left over lush farmland, and walk gently up to Bwlch y Groes. Continue down the road as far as a signed bridleway on the right **D**, and here leave the lane for a lovely grassy trail flanked by heather, bracken, bilberry, intermittent gorse and myriad wild flowers.

Follow the bridleway across the hill slope to intercept another bridleway

Beautiful springtime sunshine over the lower slopes of Llantysilio Mountain

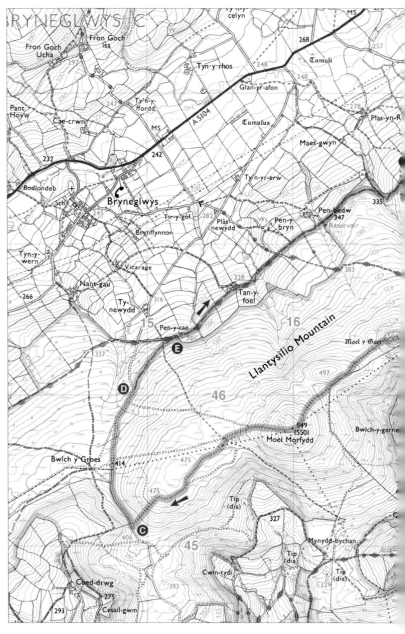

running beside an intake fence. Close by, pass through a gate/stile **E**, and then continue across rough pasture to another gate/stile, beyond which a grassy path runs beside a fence and past Tan-y-foel farm. Press on, following the bridleway across numerous pastures, always roughly parallel with a fence on the left.

The path continues easily across heather moorland, accompanied either by a fence or a wall. When the wall and the on-going bridleway diverge **F**, stay with the latter to meet a fence above the top edge of a quarry **G**. Here, the onward route lies over a fence and

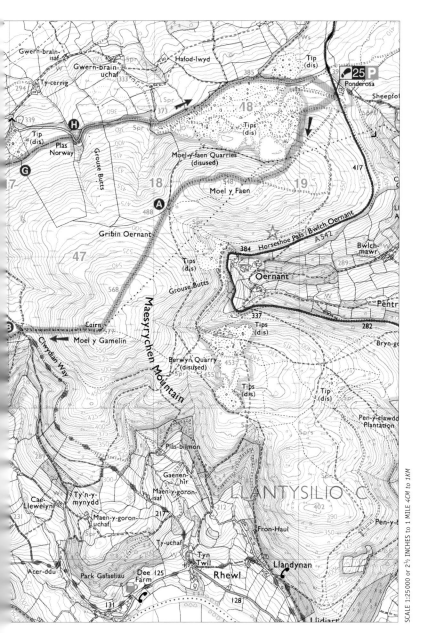

directly above the quarry, but a safer option keeps a little more distant from the quarry boundary. Both ways involve striding over a low fence, and then pressing on towards the concealed cottage at Plas Norway. The bridleway underfoot steers you towards the cottage, but you will need to move left to locate a gate **H** giving onto a narrow lane.

Turn right, up the lane, passing Plas Norway, and then simply follow the lane, past the Moel-y-faen quarries back towards the Ponderosa; the final section of the lane can be shortcut by a clear path through heather. ●

Castell Dinas Bran and Valle Crucis Abbey

		GPS waypoints	
Start	Llangollen	🥾	SJ 215 421
Distance	8¾ miles (14km)	Ⓐ	SJ 223 430
Height gain	1,965 feet (600m)	Ⓑ	SJ 227 432
Approximate time	5 hours	Ⓒ	SJ 215 458
Parking	Car parks in Llangollen	Ⓓ	SJ 208 458
Route terrain	Farmland and waterside paths; lanes	Ⓔ	SJ 205 441
		Ⓕ	SJ 203 439
Ordnance Survey maps	Landrangers 117 (Chester & Wrexham) and 125 (Bala and Lake Vyrnwy), Explorers 255 (Llangollen & Berwyn) and 256 (Wrexham & Llangollen)	Ⓖ	SJ 194 436

This is one of the great classic walks of North Wales with stunning views of the Vale of Llangollen and the Berwyn Mountains, plus plenty of scenic variety and considerable historic interest. Initially there is a steep climb to the scanty remains of Castell Dinas Bran, a superb viewpoint above Llangollen, followed by a rather easier descent and a lovely walk below the limestone cliffs of Eglwyseg, curving round to the substantial ruins of Valle Crucis Abbey. The route continues over Velvet Hill to the Horseshoe Falls on the River Dee, and the final stretch is a relaxing stroll through the valley along the towpath of the Shropshire Union Canal.

🖊 The walk begins at the south end Llangollen Bridge. Cross the bridge, turn right and then turn left up Wharf Hill, crossing the canal bridge, to reach a T-junction. Go up the steps ahead, at a public footpath sign to Offa's Dyke Path Link and walk along an enclosed path. The first part of the walk to the castle is all uphill. Cross a track by school buildings, continue along a steadily ascending path and, after passing through a kissing-gate, the going becomes steeper as you keep along the right edge of a field to another

kissing-gate.

Go through, continue along a track, keep ahead at a crossroads, go through a kissing-gate and bear right. The route continues across a flat, grassy plateau before the final, steep, zigzag pull up to the summit of the conical hill crowned by the scanty remains of Castell Dinas Bran Ⓐ. There was originally a prehistoric hillfort on the site but the present ruins are those of a 13th-century castle established by the princes of Powys. The magnificent views more than compensate for the

Valle Crucis Abbey

effort; they include the Berwyn Mountains, Eglwyseg Cliffs and Llangollen, and extend along the Dee Valley to the Pontcysyllte Aqueduct and across the English border into Shropshire.

Walk east from the castle, roughly in-line with the River Dee, to find a stony path dropping through the ramparts to a kissing-gate (waymarked Clwydian Way). Once through this, the grassy path descends the steep hillside to reach a kissing-gate into a lane, along which turn left. Cross the cattle-grid **B** and turn left, a National Trail logo (acorn) confirming the route of Offa's Dyke Path. Remain on this undulating lane, which traces the foot of the towering limestone scarp face of Creigiau Eglwyseg for the next 1¼ miles. Pass by two farms and then a road (signed Llangollen) coming in from the left. About 150yds past this

junction, fork left along a rough farm road, go through a gate and walk down to a point immediately before a steel barn. Look carefully for a stile just to the right of this (off the grassy track), cross it and trace the left-edge of the long, sloping field to a corner stile. Cross the flat bridge here and continue along the left edge of a field and just before reaching the corner, bear right and head across to a footpath post. Go through a gap in a line of trees, keep by a wire fence on the left and go through a metal gate to rejoin the lane.

Bear left, take the first turning on the left **C** and after ½ mile – where the lane descends to a farm and bends right – bear left on to a track, at a public footpath sign **D** to Valle Crucis Abbey. This firm access track passes remote cottages as it undulates along the side of the Eglwyseg valley, eventually passing above thick conifers and below superb oakwoods, giving lovely walking. At a fingerpost for Valle Crucis keep right, descending to a ladder-stile. Climb it, keep ahead and in front of a cottage turn left over another ladder-stile. Walk along the right edge of a field (ignoring a stile and waymark for Velvet Hill) to a corner. Cross a stile and a few strides ahead, turn right and descend a flight of steps **E** to a footbridge over the River Eglwyseg. Cross it, continue through a caravan site, picking up a track, and go through a gate on to a tarmac drive.

To the left are the beautiful ruins of Valle Crucis Abbey, the finest in North Wales, a Cistercian monastery founded in 1201 by the princes of Powys. Much of the church survives, including the fine west front and east end. Among the other buildings grouped around the cloister, the elegantly vaulted chapter house is particularly outstanding.

Walk along the drive, passing in front of the abbey, and where it bears left, keep ahead through a kissing-gate, at a public footpath sign to Velvet Hill, and head diagonally across a field. Go through a kissing-gate in the far corner, turn left along a road, carefully cross it and in 100yds take the steep path **F** right, signed for Llantysilio church. Climb through thick bracken and over a stile into the National Trust's Velvet Hill property, to reach a fingerpost. Keep left here, initially alongside a fence and simply favour the level path, which contours around the hillside before gradually descending as an occasionally narrow and crumbling path through bracken to a stile into birch woods. Take this and drop down to a lane at a junction.

Turn right along the wider lane (not the narrow option sharp right), shortly signed for Llantysilio and Rhewl and pass above the parking and picnic area at Llantysilio Green. The lane rises easily, revealing fine views across the

Horseshoe Falls and the wooded valley of the Dee. At a fingerpost for 'Canal' **G**, turn left down the driveway to Llantysilio church, joining a well-walked path immediately left of the lychgate. The 15th-century church is, sadly, usually locked. The path falls to a riverside section, passing beside the Horseshoe Falls. This curving weir, engineered by Thomas Telford, was constructed in 1806 to divert water into the new Llangollen branch of the

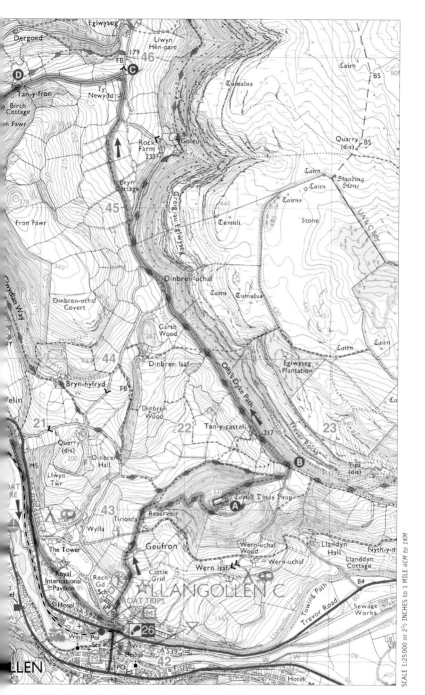

Shropshire Union Canal system. A metal gate by the gauge house gives access to a waterside path, which is followed for a tranquil 2-mile stretch back to Llangollen. On reaching Llangollen Wharf, fork right at a bollard down a tarred path, descending to the main road above the railway station. Turn left and then cross the Dee Bridge to return to the town centre. ●

Bwlch Maen Gwynedd

		GPS waypoints
Start	Llandrillo	
Distance	7¾ miles (12.5km)	☑ SJ 035 371
Height gain	2,040 feet (620m)	Ⓐ SJ 037 369
Approximate time	5 hours	Ⓑ SJ 042 352
Parking	Car park at start	Ⓒ SJ 076 341
Route terrain	Mountain moorland and farmland	Ⓓ SJ 051 375
Ordnance Survey maps	Landranger 125 (Bala & Lake Vyrnwy), Explorer 255 (Llangollen & Berwyn)	

The walk leads through austere and remote terrain, into the heart of the Berwyn Mountains, to Bwlch Maen Gwynedd, a gap in the ridge linking Cadair Bronwen and Cadair Berwyn. Bwlch Maen Gwynedd itself is at 2,342 feet (714m), and from it the views along the ridge and down into adjacent valleys, are inspirational. On the outward route some path sections are indistinct but improving, and you need to avoid a boggy area. The return uses a much clearer and easier track, but the entire walk involves rough walking across mountain moorland and hillside, and should not be attempted in poor visibility, unless you are an experienced hill walker able to navigate competently.

Llandrillo is attractively situated on the Afon Ceidiog, a tributary of the River Dee, and from the bridge there is a fine view of the tower and spire of the church rising above the village.

🖊 From the car park entrance turn left along the main road. Cross to the village hall (Y Ganolfan) and take the waymarked path passing to the right of the building. Cross a stile and walk along an enclosed path, and shortly keep ahead along the right-hand edge of a field. From an offset hedge corner and oak tree, look left to locate a stile and fingerpost next to a field gate; join a lane here Ⓐ.

Turn right along the lane, go through a gate and start a gradual climb, passing to the left of Llechwedd farmhouse and up a green track to a field gate at the foot of woodland. Join the track beyond this, skirting the woods and passing through another gate. At a junction bear left, taking a wooden gate and rising along the track to a fork. Keep left here; the track steepens before emerging from the woods at a sharp left bend. On the right here are two gates; take the lower one and follow the old sunken lane as it rises gradually towards the high moors.

Go through a gate Ⓑ and, a few paces farther on, climb a stone stile beside a gate at the border of Open Access country – there's also a bridleway signpost for Craig Berwyn here and a National Nature Reserve board for Y Berwyn Reserve. Walk ahead on the declining track, with a wall on your right. The next half mile or so may be waterlogged in places. The track descends towards a stream (Clochnant); at this stage it is important to bear left away from the stream in order to avoid a marshy area ahead, Gwern Wynodl.

The path tends to peter out here, but aim for the higher, drier, heathery moorland to the left, later bearing right back towards the stream and making for the distinct landmark of a small, rectangular conifer wood clearly seen ahead. Head towards it, and then continue to a gate. Keep forward, passing along the right edge of the conifer plantation, ford a stream and continue along a clear and obvious path that climbs gently above Clochnant. Ahead is an impressive view looking towards the head of the valley and the Berwyn ridge. At a fork take the right-hand, lower path, ford a tributary stream and continue uphill. The path briefly becomes boggy again and this is quite a tiring part of the walk, but you eventually reach a gate at the top of the pass, Bwlch Maen Gwynedd, 2,342ft (714m) high **Ⓒ**.

Go through and keep ahead a few yards to enjoy a magnificent view: to the right along the Berwyn ridge to Cadair Berwyn, to the left along the ridge to Cadair Bronwen, behind to the Dee valley, and ahead along the steep-sided, sweeping, curving valley of Cwm Maen Gwynedd. Turn back through the

Moel Ty-uchaf stone circle

gate, retrace your steps for about 100yds to a fork – probably not noticed on the way up – and take the right-hand path which can be seen heading up over the slopes in front. The path descends initially, then continues gently up, later bearing right and curving left above the head of Blaen Trawsnant. From here there is a superb view to the left of Cadair Berwyn. Continue gently up over Moel Pearce along what has become an undulating track, joining and keeping by a fence on the right, and on arriving at two gates, go through the right-hand one. The track gradually bends right, away from the fence. Go through a gate, beyond which the track braids; your target is the plantation of fir trees ahead. Two gates take you alongside the left edge of these. After the second one, look to your right to spot a stone circle on a low hilltop. It's well worth climbing up to this to enjoy the impressive views and the excellent condition of this evocative Bronze Age monument on Moel Ty-uchaf. From here, head back down a sheep track to regain the fieldside track and walk to a corner and two gates. Use the right-hand one, walking beside a wall on your left through to several gates at a crossing of paths and tracks **D**.

The track ahead becomes tarred beyond a gate. You do not want this one, however. Instead, take the wide gate on your left and join a field road bordered by widely spaced fences and walls. Simply remain on this, going through several bridlegates and across a couple of shallow fords above woodland. At a junction fork right, downhill along a stonier track. Pass through another gate to reach a junction near a farmhouse. Keep ahead here, passing above the house on a wide path beside a wall and within the edge of oak woods. A final gate leads to the

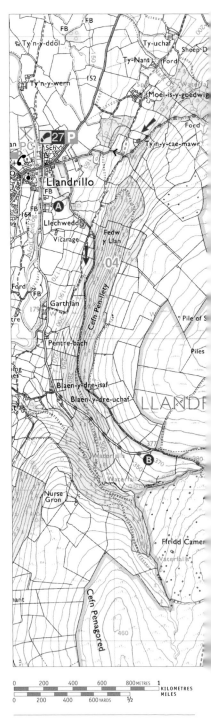

top of a steep tarred lane; following this brings you back to Llandrillo's war memorial near the village hall. ●

5000 or 2½ INCHES to 1 MILE *4CM to 1KM*

Snowdon from Rhyd Ddu

		GPS waypoints
Start	The path starts from the car park a little south of Rhyd Ddu village on the A4085 Beddgelert-Caernarfon road, and adjacent to the Rhyd Ddu station on the Welsh Highland Railway	✏ SH 571 526 Ⓐ SH 582 524 Ⓑ SH 597 537 Ⓒ SH 606 538 Ⓓ SH 609 542 Ⓔ SH 605 536 Ⓕ SH 605 521
Distance	7¾ miles (12.4km)	
Height gain	2,790 feet (850m)	
Approximate time	5 hours	
Parking	Car park at start (Pay and Display)	
Route terrain	Moorland; rough mountain pasture; rocky tracks and paths; steep cliffs	
Ordnance Survey maps	Landranger 115 (Snowdon/Yr Wyddfa), Explorer OL17 (Snowdon/Yr Wyddfa)	

The ascent of Snowdon (Yr Wyddfa) from Rhyd Ddu is arguably the easiest of the ascents, but 'easy' needs to be treated with respect. This is, after all, the highest mountain in England and Wales, and, in spite of its popularity, is no pushover. The way up from Rhyd Ddu, however, is most agreeable, and displays a side of the mountain that few bother with. The simplest expedient for the return is to retrace the outward steps. But this walk takes a different way down, one that is tricky in places, and should be avoided by anyone who is uncomfortable in airy places.

✏ From the car park walk briefly alongside the railway line, and then turn right through a gate and along a well-defined track. On your left is a small round tower, formerly the powder house for disused Ffridd Slate Quarry.

When the track divides, bear right, climbing gently as the track passes between the waste tip and the ruined buildings of the quarry. Cross a stile and soon reach a gate/stile with views to your right of Llyn y Gadair and Y Garn in the distance. The track beyond the stile bends to the left, bringing into view Llyn Cwellyn in the valley to your left. Presently the route arrives at

another gate/stile with an easily missed sign on the rock opposite: 'Snowdon, first gate on left'. Just beyond this point, the path bears to the left Ⓐ. The track in front of you is the old miners' route to the slate quarries at Bwlch Cwm Llan, below Yr Aran, and it is the route used in the descent.

Pass through a gate and cross a stream. The path continues to climb gently, and gradually broadens. The landscape is now one of tangled heather and rock, through which the path leads to another stile with sheep pens to the left of the path. On your right is the wide expanse of Cwm Caregog bounded

Some fine rocky ridge work along Allt Maenderyn

on the far side by Allt Maenderyn, a fine, narrow ridge used on the descent. The path soon becomes steeper and rougher underfoot.

Onward, the path crosses a stream, and climbs steeply until it reaches a wall. This section of the path is straightforward, but is bouldery and uneven. Through a gate in the wall, the path emerges onto the shoulder of Llechog. From here, the view is across Cwm Clogwyn and through Bwlch Cwm Brwynog, flanked by Moel Cynghorion, on the left, and Clogwyn Du'r Arddu, and down towards Llanberis.

Continuing to the right, the path climbs the Llechog ridge through a harsh landscape, one susceptible to the prevailing wind. This is a stark and lovely landscape dominated by frost-shattered rocks; what little vegetation there is, is low growing and stunted.

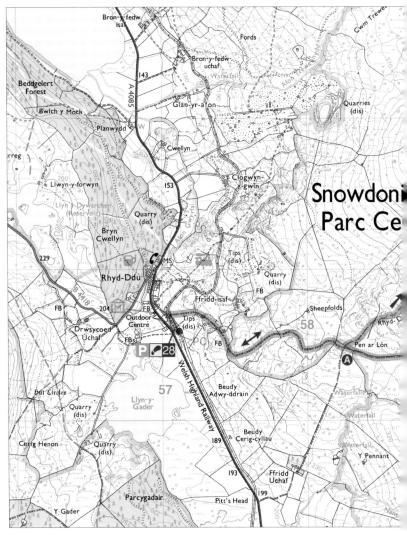

Soon, you reach a wall on the right **B**, from beside which there is a superb view into Cwm Clogwyn, housing three tiny lakes, Llyn Nadroedd (Lake of the Snakes), Llyn Coch (Red Lake) and Llyn Glas (Blue Lake). This wild and lovely cwm is typical of those gouged by glacial action during the last Ice Age, but few in North Wales are as awesome as this.

Continue along the ridge. [NOTE: In winter conditions, this final section to the summit is for experienced and properly equipped mountaineers only.]

After passing an impressive scree slope on the left, the route comes to the beginning of Bwlch Main, also known as the 'Saddle'. Bwlch Main **C** is a narrow col, and is extremely exposed to the wind. It is safe, in reasonable conditions, provided you keep to the path.

The final section to the top of Snowdon is steep and unrelenting. The path soon starts to climb steeply again and meets the Watkin Path coming from the right at a solitary marker stone **D**. The summit is only a few minutes climb away up a gentle but bouldery slope.

SCALE 1:25000 or 2½ INCHES to 1 MILE 4CM to 1KM

From the summit, retreat to the finger of rock and Bwlch Main, but then continue along a ridge path, initially in a south-westerly direction. When the path forks **E**, the quick way back bears right, retracing the outward route. For a more sensational return, bear left at this point, uphill, to experience some fine rocky ridge work along Allt Maenderyn. There are a few awkward, scrambly stretches along this steadily descending ridge. This is no place to hurry, and can be very tiring, but it is hugely satisfying.

Eventually, the route arrives at a ladder-stile spanning a fence, beyond which a final, rocky staircase of slate leads to Bwlch Cwm Llan **F**, where the remains of old slate quarries are evident. At this point, turn abruptly right (west), following a clear path that feeds into a broadening track, originally used to transport slate. Follow this steadily downwards until the outward route is rejoined, and then followed back to Rhyd Ddu.

Further Information

 ## *Safety on the Hills*

The hills, mountains and moorlands of Britain, though of modest height compared with those in many other countries, need to be treated with respect. Friendly and inviting in good weather, they can quickly be transformed into wet, misty, windswept and potentially dangerous areas of wilderness in bad weather. Even on an outwardly fine and settled summer day, conditions can rapidly deteriorate at high altitudes and, in winter, even more so.

Therefore it is advisable always to take both warm and waterproof clothing, sufficient nourishing food, a hot drink, first-aid kit, torch and whistle. Wear suitable footwear, such as strong walking boots or shoes that give a good grip over rocky terrain and on slippery slopes. Try to obtain a local weather forecast and bear it in mind before you start. Do not be afraid to abandon your proposed route and return to your starting point in the event of a sudden and unexpected deterioration in the weather. Do not go alone and allow enough time to finish the walk well before nightfall.

Most of the walks described in this book do not venture into remote wilderness areas and will be safe to do, given due care and respect, at any time of year in all but the most unreasonable weather. Indeed, a crisp, fine winter day often provides perfect walking conditions, with firm ground underfoot and a clarity that is not possible to achieve in the other seasons of the year. A few walks, however, are suitable only for reasonably fit and experienced hill walkers able to use a compass and should definitely not be tackled by anyone else during the winter months or in bad weather, especially high winds and mist. These are indicated in the general description that precedes each of the walks.

 ## *Walkers and the Law*

The Countryside and Rights of Way Act (CRoW Act 2000) extends the rights of access previously enjoyed by walkers in England and Wales. Implementation of these rights began on 19 September 2004. The Act amends existing legislation and for the first time provides access on foot to certain types of land – defined as mountain, moor, heath, down and registered common land.

Where You Can Go
Rights of Way
Prior to the introduction of the CRoW Act, walkers could only legally access the countryside along public rights of way. These are either 'footpaths' (for walkers only) or 'bridleways' (for walkers, riders on horseback and pedal cyclists). A third category called 'Byways open to all traffic' (BOATs), is used by motorised vehicles as well as those using non-mechanised transport. Mainly they are green lanes, farm and estate roads, although occasionally they will be found crossing mountainous area.

Rights of way are marked on Ordnance Survey maps. Look for the green broken lines on the Explorer maps, or the red dashed lines on Landranger maps.

The term 'right of way' means exactly what it says. It gives a right of passage over what, for the most part, is private land. Under pre-CRoW legislation walkers were required to keep to the line of the right of way and not stray onto land on either side. If you did inadvertently wander off the right of way, either because of faulty map reading or because the route was not clearly indicated on the ground, you were technically trespassing.

Local authorities have a legal obligation to ensure that rights of way are kept clear and free of obstruction, and are signposted where they leave metalled roads. The duty of local authorities to install signposts extends to the placing of signs along a path or way, but only where the authority considers it necessary to have a signpost or waymark to assist persons unfamiliar with the locality.

The New Access Rights
Access Land
As well as being able to walk on existing rights of way, under the new legislation you now have access to large areas of open land. You can of course continue to use rights of way footpaths to cross this land, but the main difference is that you can now lawfully leave the path and wander at will, but only in areas designated as access land.

Where to Walk
 Areas now covered by the new access rights – Access Land – are shown on Ordnance Survey Explorer maps bearing the access land symbol on the front cover.

'Access Land' is shown on Ordnance Survey maps by a light yellow tint surrounded by a pale orange border. New orange coloured 'i' symbols on the maps will show the location of permanent access information boards installed by the access authorities.

Restrictions
The right to walk on access land may lawfully be restricted by landowners, but whatever restrictions are put into place on access land they have no effect on existing rights of way, and you can continue to walk on them.

Dogs
Dogs can be taken on access land, but must be kept on leads of two metres or less between 1 March and 31 July, and at all times where they are near livestock. In addition land-owners may impose a ban on all dogs from fields where lambing takes place for up to six weeks in any year. Dogs may be banned from moorland used for grouse shooting and breeding for up to five years.

General Obstructions
Obstructions can sometimes cause a problem on a walk and the most common

of these is where the path across a field has been ploughed over. It is legal for a farmer to plough up a path provided that it is restored within two weeks. This does not always happen and you are faced with the dilemma of following the line of the path, even if this means treading on crops, or walking round the edge of the field. Although the latter course of action seems the most sensible, it does mean that you would be trespassing.

Other obstructions can vary from overhanging vegetation to wire fences across the path, locked gates or even a cattle feeder on the path.

Use common sense. If you can get round the obstruction without causing damage, do so. Otherwise only remove as much of the obstruction as is necessary to secure passage.

If the right of way is blocked and cannot be followed, there is a long-standing view that in such circumstances there is a right to deviate, but this cannot wholly be relied on. Although it is accepted in law that highways (and that includes rights of way) are for the public service, and if the usual track is impassable, it is for the general good that people should be entitled to pass into another line. However, this should not be taken as indicating a right to deviate when-ever a way is impassable. If in doubt, retreat.

Report obstructions to the local authority and/or the Ramblers.

 ## Useful Organisations

Campaign for National Parks
5-11 Lavington Street, London, SE1 0NZ
Tel. 020 7981 2800
www.cnp.org.uk

Campaign for the Protection of Rural Wales
Ty Gwyn, 31 High Street, Welshpool,
Powys SY21 7YD
Tel. 01938 552525/556212
www.cprw.org.uk

Countryside Council for Wales
Maes-y-Ffynnon, Penrhosgarnedd,
Bangor, Gwynedd, LL57 2DW

Tel. 0845 130 6229
www.ccw.gov.uk

Forestry Commission Wales
Welsh Government, Rhodfa Padarn,
Llanbadarn Fawr, Aberystwyth,
Ceredigion SY23 3UR
Tel. 0300 068 0300
www.forestry.gov.uk

Long Distance Walkers' Association
www.ldwa.org.uk

National Trust (Wales Regional Office)
Trinity Square, Llandudno, Conwy LL30 2DE
Tel: 01492 860123
www.nationaltrust.org.uk

North Wales Tourism
77 Conway Road, Colwyn Bay LL29 7LN
Tel. 01492 531731
www.gonorthwales.co.uk

Ordnance Survey
Tel. 03456 05 05 05 (Lo-call)
www.ordnancesurvey.co.uk

Ramblers' Wales
3 Coopers Yard, Curran Road, Cardiff
CF10 5NB
Tel. 029 2064 4308
www.ramblers.org.uk/wales

Snowdonia National Park Authority
National Park Office, Penrhyndeudraeth,
Gwynedd LL48 6LF
Tel. 01766 770274
www.snowdonia-npa.gov.uk

National Park Information Centres:
Aberdyfi: 01654 767321
Beddgelert: 01766 890615
Betws-y-Coed: 01690 710426
Dolgellau: 01341 422888
Harlech: 01766 780658

Snowdonia Society
Caban, Brynrefail, Caernarfon,
Gwynedd LL55 3NR
Tel. 01286 685498
www.snowdonia-society.org.uk

Tourist Information
Wales Tourist Board
www.visitwales.com

Local Tourist Information Centres:
Bala: 01678 521021
Bangor: 01248 352768
Betws-y-Coed: 01690 710426
Blaenau Ffestiniog: 01766 830360
Caernarfon: 01286 672232
Colwyn Bay: 01492 531731
Conwy: 01492 592248
Dolgellau: 01341 422888
Llanberis: 01286 870765
Llandudno: 01492 577577
Mold: 01352 759331
Porthmadog: 01766 512981
Pwllheli: 01758 613000
Rhyl: 01745 355068
Wrexham: 01978 292015

Youth Hostels Association
Trevelyan House, Dimple Road, Matlock,
Derbyshire DE4 3YH
Tel. 0800 019 1700 (reservations)
www.yha.org.uk

Ordnance Survey maps for North Wales and Snowdonia

North Wales and Snowdonia are covered by
Ordnance Survey 1:50 000 (11/4 inches to 1
mile or 2cm to 1km) scale Landranger map
sheets 115, 116, 117, 123, 124, 125 and
126. These all-purpose maps are packed
with information to help you explore the
area and show viewpoints, picnic sites,
places of interest and caravan and camping
sites. To examine the area in more detail,
and especially if you are planning walks,
Ordnance Survey Explorer maps at 1:25
000 (21/2 inches to 1 mile or 4cm to 1km)
scale are ideal:

OL17 (Snowdon/Yr Wyddfa)
OL18 (Harlech, Porthmadog & Bala)
OL23 (Cadair Idris & Llyn Tegid)
240 (Oswestry)
253 (Lleyn Peninsula West)
254 (Lleyn Peninsula East)
255 (Llangollen & Berwyn)
256 (Wrexham & Llangollen)
264 (Vale of Clwyd)
265 (Clwydian Range)
266 (Wirral & Chester)

Text:	Terry Marsh
Photography:	Terry Marsh, Crimson Publishing, and on p48 Dave Newbould
Editorial:	Ark Creative (UK) Ltd
Design:	Ark Creative (UK) Ltd

 This product includes mapping data licensed from Ordnance Survey® with the permission of the Controller of Her Majesty's Stationery Office. © Crown Copyright 2015. All rights reserved. Licence number 150002047. Ordnance Survey, the OS symbol and Pathfinder are registered trademarks and Explorer, Landranger and Outdoor Leisure are trademarks of the Ordnance Survey, the national mapping agency of Great Britain.

ISBN: 978-1-7805-9072-1

While every care has been taken to ensure the accuracy of the route directions, the publishers cannot accept responsibility for errors or omissions, or for changes in details given. The countryside is not static: hedges and fences can be removed, stiles can become gates, field boundaries can alter, footpaths can be rerouted and changes in ownership can result in the closure or diversion of some concessionary paths. Also, paths that are easy and pleasant for walking in fine conditions may become slippery, muddy and difficult in wet weather, while stepping stones across rivers and streams may become impassable.

If you find an inaccuracy in either the text or maps, please write to Crimson Publishing at the address below.

First published 1998 by Jarrold Publishing
Revised and reprinted 2001, 2004, 2006, 2007, 2009

This new edition first published in Great Britain in 2015 by Crimson Publishing, 19-21C Charles Street, Bath, BA1 1HX

www.pathfinderwalks.co.uk

Printed in Singapore. 7/15

A catalogue record for this book is available from the British Library.

Front cover: Heathery hillsides near Cwm Bychan
Page 1: Chirk castle

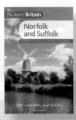

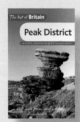